Lexington, Virginia and the Civil War

Lexington, Virginia and the Civil War

Richard G. Williams Jr.

The History Press

Published by The History Press
Charleston, SC 29403
www.historypress.net

First published 2013

Manufactured in the United States

ISBN 978.1.60949.391.2

Library of Congress CIP data applied for.

Notice: The information in this book is true and complete to the best of our knowledge. It is offered without guarantee on the part of the author or The History Press. The author and The History Press disclaim all liability in connection with the use of this book.

This book is dedicated to the memory of Jim Lewis.

Contents

Banks Smither and the rest of the good folks at The History Press have been more than accommodating as I suffered through a computer virus and crash and extended deadlines. I also want to thank the Sons of Confederate Veterans, the United Daughters of the Confederacy, the Stonewall Jackson House, the Virginia Military Institute, the Rockbridge Historical Society, the Rockbridge Civil War Roundtable, Washington and Lee University and Lee Chapel for their outstanding work in preserving and promoting Lexington's rich history. The individuals who work behind the scenes in these organizations and institutions rarely receive the accolades and recognition they so richly deserve. Without their efforts and sacrifices, Lexington's history would be lost.

I also need to thank my wife for her patience as I, once again, spent countless hours hunkered down in my basement office surrounded by the ghosts of Lee, Jackson, Jim Lewis, Robert Price, Francis Smith, Maggie Preston and so many others, not to mention mountains of books and files. She is the bride of my youth, and her price is far above rubies. Finally, I thank God for the privilege of being one of His and for giving me the love of history, as well as the desire to share it.

Introduction

My earliest memories of Lexington, Virginia, come from an elementary school field trip in 1968, when I was in the fourth grade. Fourth-grade students in Virginia at that time were required to study Virginia history, and the commonwealth thought learning Virginia's history was so important to its future that students were required to repeat the study of Virginia history again in the seventh grade. That trip in 1968 involved a tour of Lee Chapel, as well as Jackson Memorial Hall and VMI Museum on the campus of the Virginia Military Institute. I recall the enthusiasm of the tour guides as they regaled their wide-eyed young audience with tales of heritage, heroism and a proud history.

I drank it all in, though I was no stranger to Civil War history. Just two years earlier, Walt Disney had released *Mosby's Marauders*, a romanticized version of Confederate colonel John Singleton Mosby's daring escapades in Virginia. I became an immediate and ardent fan. And since I was born and raised in Virginia's Shenandoah Valley, I was surrounded by the history of the War Between the States. In school during history class, weekly on television, historical highway markers, the names of roads and schools, my Confederate great-great-grandfather's musket that hung in my grandparent's home, the images of Lee and Jackson that hung on the wall over my father's desk—I was immersed daily in the history of our nations bloodiest conflict.

Yet as I experienced Lexington for the first time that day in 1968, even at such a young age I realized there was something particularly special about *that* place. From the locks of George Washington's and Robert E. Lee's hair carefully preserved at the Lee Chapel Museum, to Stonewall Jackson's stuffed horse, Little Sorrel, proudly displayed at the VMI Museum, I began to understand the importance of preserving and studying history, especially the history of the Civil War, which so dramatically impacted my home and ancestors. Of course, this was part of the reason our class visited Lexington. And it is the reason for this book. Though this work breaks no new ground, it is my hope that it will, in some small way, encourage in its readers what a ten year-old-boy experienced in Lexington some forty-five years ago.

Richard G. Williams Jr.
January 19, 2013
Huckleberry Hollow, Virginia

Chapter 1

Peace in the Valley

In those piping days of peace nature never looked more lovely, the blue mountains and green fields of old Rockbridge never more beautiful; all nature seemed to be at peace.
—Alexander Tedford Barclay, Liberty Hall Volunteers

One cannot fully understand Lexington, Virginia, without some understanding of the valley landscape and geography that has cradled it for almost two and a half centuries, as well as the people who inhabit it. Virginia's Shenandoah Valley is a place of beauty, history and legend. Known during the War Between the States as the "Breadbasket of the Confederacy," its fertile soils and hardy citizens nourished the ill-fated Confederacy for much of the war. It comprises one of the richest agricultural regions in the eastern United States. As historian Kenneth Koons has noted:

> *By the mid-nineteenth century, farmers of the Shenandoah Valley (defined here as comprising the counties of Frederick, Clarke, Shenandoah, Warren, Rockingham, Page, Augusta, Rockbridge, and Botetourt) worked only nine percent of the improved acres of farmland in Virginia but produced twenty-two percent of the Commonwealth's wheat crop. By this time, the Valley had emerged as one of the most productive wheat farming regions of the South. One historian's comparison of wheat productivity in ten multi-county regions of the South encompassing portions of Virginia, Tennessee, Kentucky, Missouri, and Georgia, shows that in 1850 farmers in a four-*

> *county portion of the Shenandoah Valley—the counties of Rockbridge, Augusta, Rockingham, and Page—produced almost twenty bushels of wheat per capita, while farmers of the other nine regions produced fewer than six bushels per capita.*

Rockingham County remains, even today, one of the top one hundred counties in the United States for agricultural production.

Though its ground has been soaked with the blood of Native Americans, explorers, pioneers, British and colonial soldiers, as well as Civil War soldiers, to those who know it, "peaceful and pastoral" would be the words that most often come to mind when someone mentions the "Daughter of the Stars." Legend says this is the name given to the valley by Native Americans centuries before the white man first crossed the Blue Ridge Mountains and laid eyes on the vast expanse of grasslands, crystal-clear streams and forests teeming with game.

Tucked between the Blue Ridge mountain range to the east and the Alleghany mountain range to the west, its northern (lower) and southern (upper) borders extend roughly from Harpers Ferry and the Potomac River in the north to Buchanan, Virginia, in the south—almost 180 miles. One of the valley's most prominent landmarks—the Shenandoah River—divides much of the lower valley as it flows south to north before meeting the Potomac at Harpers Ferry; hence, the "lower" and "upper" references.

It is one of the most historic areas of the United States—hunted for hundreds of years by the Shawnee, Monacan, Iroquois, Occoneechee and Piscataway; surveyed by George Washington; settled by the Scots-Irish and Germans; and the backdrop for what some consider the greatest military campaign in American history: Stonewall Jackson's legendary "Valley Campaign." It is a land of storied tales and legends, of unmatched beauty and abundant wildlife, of loyalty and tragedy, of romance and death. Those who visit it never want to leave. Those who leave it always yearn to come back. When the English first arrived on Virginia soil in the 1600s, Native Americans told them of a land to the west that contained vast herds

Alexander Tedford Barclay, Liberty Hall Volunteers, circa 1866–67. *Special Collections, Leyburn Library, Washington and Lee University.*

The Shenandoah Valley, by William Sonntag, circa 1860.

of buffalo and endless woodlands of hardwood trees, including the mighty chestnut, some over six hundred years old and one hundred feet tall. For centuries, the Shenandoah Valley had served as the Native Americans' most fertile hunting grounds. Such tales were received with skepticism among many of the English, but the natives were not exaggerating.

Nineteenth-century author William Alexander Caruthers described what Governor Alexander Spotswood and the Knights of the Golden Horseshoe first saw and experienced as they came across the Blue Ridge and their eyes fell on the valley of the Shenandoah:

> *What a panorama there burst upon the enraptured vision of the assembled young chivalry of Virginia! Never did the eye of mortal man rest upon a more magnificent scene! The vale beneath looked like a great sea of vegetation in the moon-light, rising and falling in undulating and picturesque lines, as far as the eye could reach towards the north-east and south-west; but their vision was interrupted on the opposite side by the Alleghanies* [sic]. *For hours the old veteran chief stood on the identical spot which he first occupied, drinking in rapture from the vision which he beheld. Few words were spoken by any one, after the first exclamations of surprise and enthusiasm were over. The scene was too overpowering—the grand solitudes, the sublime*

stillness, gave rise to profound emotions which found no utterance. Nearly everyone wandered off and seated himself upon some towering crag, and then held communion with the silent spirit of the place. There lay the valley of Virginia, that garden spot of the earth, in its first freshness and purity, as it came from the hands of its Maker. Not a white man had ever trod that virgin soil, from the beginning of the world. What a solemn and sublime temple of nature was there—and who could look upon it, as it spread far out to the east and west, until it was lost in the dim and hazy horizon, and not feel deeply impressed with the majesty of its Author.

Almost one hundred years later, Lexingtonian and writer Henry Boley offered his own description of this "garden spot of the earth":

The Valley of Virginia! A magic name to add to "Tidewater Virginia, the chateaux of France, the castles of the Rhine, the Bay of Naples, the canals of Venice, the lakes of Killarney and the Spanish Main." The Valley of Virginia is not only an expectation and promise, but a realization and a fulfillment. At any season of the year it is a place of beauty, whether its hills, vales and mountains are seen under a blanket of snow or in the very early springtime, clad in apple blossoms, dogwood, azaleas, redbud, and many other blossoming trees and shrubs, bounded on all sides by the bluest of blue mountains; or later in the summer, when the grains and grasses in great variety are being harvested and stacked, it never fails to present a happy and satisfying sight. The very name, Valley of the Shenandoah, means home and loved ones to countless thousands throughout the world, who trace their ancestry, if not to their very own childhood days, to this favored spot.

Though both Caruthers's and Boley's descriptions are from another time, they remain, in many ways, accurate to this day. It was here in the Shenandoah Valley—this "sublime temple of nature"—that the picturesque town of Lexington was birthed.

Margaret Junkin Preston, though born in Pennsylvania, is often remembered as the poetess laureate of the South. She was the sister-in-law of Stonewall Jackson and the daughter of George Junkin, who served, up to the time of the Civil War, as president of Washington College. She would marry John Thomas Lewis Preston, credited by many as the founder of the Virginia Military Institute. Some of Mrs. Preston's poetry describes how the peaceful town of Lexington would soon be transformed:

Above, left: John Thomas Lewis Preston. *VMI Archives*.

Above, right: Margaret Junkin Preston. *VMI Archives*.

She feels the hot blood of the nation beat high;
With rapture she catches the rallying cry:
From mountain, and valley and hamlet they come!
On every side echoes the roll of the drum.
As people as firm, as united, as bold—
As ever drew blade for the blessings they hold,
Step sternly and solemnly forth in their might,
And swear on their altars to die for the right.

Resting in the upper (southern) portion of the Shenandoah Valley, Lexington is certainly the most historic of the valley's communities. Rockbridge County was created by the Virginia legislature in 1778. First known as Gilbert Campbell's Ford, the legislature named Lexington as the county seat after the first battle of America's War of Independence. The town originally consisted of twenty acres and was laid out with three of its streets running north to south. These were Randolph, Main and Jefferson. The other three, named Henry, Washington and Nelson, run east to west. Five of the six streets were named in honor of Virginia statesmen from America's struggle for independence.

Colonel John Thomas Lewis Preston (Stonewall Jackson's brother-in-law by Jackson's first marriage) described what Lexington—this "Athens of the Old South" and "God-favored place"—was like in 1816:

> *The town was in about the same limits decreed in 1777. Main Street was not compactly built up. The finest structure was the Ann Smith Academy and beyond it were corn fields. On each side of the college* [Washington College] *were two brick halls, two stories high. Water was from the pump and from the back spring and hawling* [sic] *water by sleds was quite an institution. Ice houses were unknown. The Presbyterian was the only church, with two services on Sabbath, separated by an "intervale" of one-half hour and both were well attended. A large oak grove extended from the church gate to Wood's Creek and this was a rambling ground during the intermission.*

In 1936, Henry Boley described the people who were the earliest to inhabit Lexington:

> *They were of upright lives, high standards, and fearless in the pursuit of religious and intellectual freedom, unafraid of hard work, which they considered an honorable means to an end…Their distinguishing peculiarities were very pronounced, and some are noticeable in their descendants today. They remain a praying people, and so afraid of God that they hold in their hearts no fear of man.*

Casimir Bohn engraving showing barracks and other VMI buildings as they looked in 1857. *VMI Archives.*

These early Lexington residents, mostly Scots-Irish, had migrated down the Great Wagon Road (modern-day U.S. Route 11) from Pennsylvania. The route is one of the most historic in the United States. The National Park Service makes this observation about the Great Wagon Road and its importance to the Shenandoah Valley and its history:

The Valley Pike is the story of America and American ingenuity. The evolution of a wagon road into a great artery to distant cities was part of a sweeping change that took place between the American Revolution and the Civil War and played a critical role in the development and history of the Shenandoah Valley. As settlement grew in the Shenandoah Valley, an old native trail coined the "Great Warrior Path" became known as the "Great Wagon Road." The Wagon Road began in Philadelphia and connected Lancaster, York, Gettysburg, Chambersburg, Greencastle to Winchester. Continuing South to Georgia. The Shenandoah Valley became a rich agricultural resource during the colonial period that developed in the Valley. By the 1790s the Shenandoah Valley had become one of the most important wheat and flour producing regions in the entire south.

And as the National Park Services makes clear, the road's importance during the Civil War cannot be overstated:

The Valley Turnpike was a road that had significant strategic importance during the Civil War. It allowed the rapid movement of armies, both men and material, over a short time. Example: The overwhelming success of Jackson's 1862 Valley Campaign heavily hinged on the rapid movement of his outnumbered forces—his repeated use of the Valley Turnpike allowed for these rapid movements.

The historic highway has even been the subject of poetry:

The Long Gray Trail

Ninety miles and more it stretches
Up the Valley, towards the south:
Firm it is to wheel and hoof beat,
Firm it holds in flood and drought:
And it links the towns and cities,
Jewels on a silver chain,

> *a long grasp for life's tangibles. From their habituation to clan warfare in the ancestral home and to battling the wild Celts of Ulster, they brought with them a fighting instinct and aggressiveness and a handiness with weapons. Given the nature of the American frontier and the general determination to advance it, regardless, they made ideal frontiersmen, to equal before long, the Redmen, whose woodcraft and dress they adopted. They were not only the new Americans, they were to be the creators of the New America.*

Kennedy further notes that "the hitherto uninhabited Shenandoah lands were a paradise to the Scots-Irish settlers, a vast fertile prairie that was both a highly productive and a healthy abode." As the Scots-Irish inhabitants of the valley grew in number and prospered, Lexington grew and prospered along with them and became an important cultural center for the Shenandoah Valley. Two institutions would become indispensable to not only the culture of Lexington but also its everlasting connection to the Civil War. Today, Washington and Lee University is a small, private, liberal arts school in Lexington and the ninth-oldest institution of higher learning in the nation. Its beginning was quite humble, as described in *Waddell's Annals of Augusta County, Virginia, from 1726 to 1871:*

> *As a part of the history of the county, we mention that the Presbytery of Hanover, about the year 1773, determined to establish "Augusta Academy," and it was at first proposed to locate the institution at Staunton. At a meeting of Presbytery, in April, 1775, persons were appointed to solicit subscriptions in behalf of the academy, among whom were William McPheeters and John Trimble, at North Mountain; Thomas Stuart and Walter Davis, at Tinkling Spring; Sampson Mathews, at Staunton; and George Mathews, George Moffett and James Allen, in Augusta congregation.*
>
> *In May, 1776, the Presbytery determined to locate the school on Timber Ridge, "as there was no one in Staunton to take the management, and it was uncertain whether there ever would be." At the same time the Rev. William Graham was elected rector, and a young man named John Montgomery his assistant. Mr. Graham was born in Pennsylvania, in 1746, and was educated at Princeton College. Mr. Montgomery was born in Augusta, and graduated at Princeton in 1775. He spent the last years of his life as pastor of Rocky Spring church, in Augusta. Trustees were also appointed: Rev. John Brown, Rev. James Waddell, Thomas and Andrew Lewis, William Preston, Sampson Mathews, Samuel McDowell, George Moffett, and others. In 1779, the school was removed to Lexington, and called "Liberty Hall."*

Liberty Hall ruins, circa 1870. *Special Collections, Leyburn Library, Washington and Lee University.*

In 1782, the Virginia legislature chartered the school as Liberty Hall Academy and empowered it to grant degrees. In 1793, a sturdy limestone building was built on a ridge overlooking Lexington. That structure was destroyed by fire in 1803. The ruins remain and are preserved today, a testament to the school's strong foundation and longevity. Prior to the fire, the school had already escaped financial destruction when, in 1796, George Washington bequeathed to it its first major endowment, which consisted of James River Canal Stock worth $20,000. Grateful for the gift, the trustees immediately changed the name of the school to Washington Academy. It would not be the last time a prominent Virginian came to the school's rescue.

In 1813, the name of the school was again changed to Washington College, and it was relocated to its present spot in Lexington. By the time the Civil War broke out, some of Washington College's students would form one of the most renowned units in the Confederate army: the Liberty Hall Volunteers. Of course, Washington College was not the only school that played a pivotal role during the American Civil War.

John Newton Lyle, Liberty Hall Volunteers, circa 1866–67. *Special Collections, Leyburn Library, Washington and Lee University.*

To any student of Civil War history, it is impossible to mention Lexington, Virginia, without thinking of "the Institute." It was in February 1816 that the Virginia General Assembly passed legislation authorizing the formation of three arsenals to warehouse and maintain the arms and munitions leftover from the War of 1812. One of these three was to be established west of the Blue Ridge Mountains. Twenty soldiers originally manned this arsenal. These soldiers, though generally well behaved, sometimes caused trouble in the peaceful town of Lexington, and the pious Lexington citizenry was unhappy with the soldiers' immoral behavior.

Despite the concerns over the soldiers' behavior, the townspeople were grateful for the security of having a military outpost so close by. This led locals to devise a plan in 1834 to "replace the soldiers with young men whose education in the customary manner was to be combined with military training and duty as the arsenal guard." Legislation to accomplish this was enacted in 1837, and Governor David Campbell appointed five distinguished men to the school's first board of visitors. In 1838, Campbell appointed two more members who included Colonel J.T.L. Preston. It was Preston who originated the name for the new school: Virginia Military Institute. "Virginia" because it was a state institution; "Military" to indicate "its characteristic feature"; and "Institute" because it was to be "something different from either a college or university."

VMI rises like a fortress on the hills above the Maury River, overlooking some of the most beautiful scenery in the Great Valley of Virginia. As a military school, VMI ranks second in age only to West Point in America, and its founders had "a keen eye for the beautiful as well as the practical." Somewhat gothic and Spartan in appearance, it is the most familiar landmark in Lexington.

Certainly, there was much more to the cultural atmosphere and influence in Lexington than its educational institutions. Christianity and

Thomas J. "Stonewall" Jackson, circa 1855. *VMI Archives.*

the local churches were at the very center of Lexington's character. By the time future Confederate general and legend Thomas J. Jackson arrived in Lexington in 1851 to accept a teaching position at VMI, the tightknit citizenry of Lexington had formed a vigorous evangelical community. The local paper would refer to Lexington and surrounding Rockbridge County as "the very home of gospel blessings." Five Christian congregations were clustered within the town limits. Inside one block were three churches: Lexington Presbyterian (1797), Randolph Street Methodist (1816) and the Lexington Baptist Church (1841). At the bottom of the hill, just a stone's throw from Washington College, was Grace Episcopal Church (Robert E. Lee Memorial Church). The Methodist Episcopal Church was then meeting in the county courthouse until a building was completed in 1853. Just outside the town limits stood the African Baptist Church, near what was then the North River (Maury River). The congregation was composed of both slaves and freedmen and was overseen by the elders of the Presbyterian Church. The community was bustling with missionary and Christian endeavors. As former graduate fellow of the Stonewall Jackson House E. Lynn Pearson has written:

> *Far from being cold and sectarian, Lexington was home to a flourishing evangelical tradition of ecumenical fellowship, prayer, and revivals, and a busy center for colporteurs, missionaries, and visiting agents from eastern benevolent societies and publishing houses. Local chapters of the American Bible Society, the American Colonization Society, and the Sons of Temperance, attracted members from all churches.*

Sadly, the closeness that marked this peaceful and picturesque valley town would soon be shattered by the drumbeats of war, and divided loyalties would strain families and friendships.

Chapter 2
Divided Loyalties

For I am come to set a man at variance against his father, and the daughter against her mother, and the daughter in law against her mother in law.
—Matthew 10:35

(Some of the information in this chapter is abridged text from *Maxims of Robert E. Lee for Young Gentlemen* and is used by permission of the publisher, Pelican Publishing Company, Inc.)

As twenty-first-century Americans, it can sometimes be difficult to understand how Southerners were able to embrace their new country and turn their back on the old Union. Our increasingly homogenized culture has forgotten the very strong chords of statehood and regionalism that influenced so many Southerners. Though Confederate general Robert E. Lee did not become a resident of Lexington until shortly after the Civil War had ended, his name is forever connected to that community. He lived his last days there and made his most lasting contribution there—as president of Washington College. The struggle he experienced due to his dedication and ties to the Union provides us with some keen insight into the mindset of not only Lee but also many of the nineteenth-century Lexingtonians who ultimately made the same decision Lee made.

Although Lee was an aristocrat from the Northern Neck area of Virginia, he was, originally—like most of his fellow citizens in western Virginia—solidly pro-Union and anti-secessionist. But Lexington, like the rest of Virginia, was not unified in its sentiments. As Stonewall Jackson's eminent biographer James I. Robertson Jr. pointed out:

> *Secession deeply split the Lexington community. The great majority of citizens in and around towns had a strong, inherited attachment for the Union. They were convinced that an adjustment could be reached and all dangers circumscribed.*

Condemning Lee—and others like him—as a traitor for fighting for the Confederacy reveals a misunderstanding of the times in which Lee lived. Those who hold to such an opinion of Lee are often substituting modern views of patriotism (love of and loyalty to a *government*) onto what was a common nineteenth-century view: love of a *land and its people*.

Lee's guiding principle was that of duty. Despite all the criticisms that have been leveled at Lee, his motivation for casting his lot with the Confederacy can in no way be viewed as selfish, whatever else it may have been. He had little to gain and everything to lose. And nowhere was Lee's commitment to duty more obvious than in its influence on his decision to decline Lincoln's offer of commander of all Union forces and to suffer the fate of his native Virginia. There could be no possible motive for glory or riches, for Lee was fully aware of the likely outcome of a struggle against the numerically and militarily superior North. He was also aware that, contrary to the opinion of many, it would be a long and bloody conflict.

After Fort Sumter, Lincoln had called on the states to provide seventy-five thousand militiamen for ninety days' service to put down the "rebellion." Robert E. Lee's native land, Virginia, answered that call with one of its own: a call for secession. The Old Dominion and cradle of liberty that had given birth to men like George Washington, Thomas Jefferson and Patrick Henry would not stand for what it viewed as heavy-handed dictates. Many Virginians likely recalled the sentiments of Thomas Jefferson, expressed in a letter penned by Jefferson to William Stephens Smith in November 1787. Jefferson's words were eerily prophetic:

> *What country ever existed a century and a half without a rebellion? And what country can preserve its liberties if their rulers are not warned from time to time that their people preserve the spirit of resistance? Let them take arms. The remedy is to set them right as to facts, pardon and pacify them. What signify a few lives lost in a century or two? The tree of liberty must*

> *be refreshed from time to time with the blood of patriots and tyrants. It is its natural manure.*

Figuratively speaking, and in the collective memory of its citizens, Virginia's soil was still moist with the blood of the British, and if necessary, additional blood would be appropriate. Yet while hotheaded rhetoric was in plentiful supply—both in newspapers and in Virginia's legislature—no one knew better than Lee what a war with the Union would entail. Yet he was torn. In a December 1860 letter to his oldest son, Custis, Lee expressed his divided emotions and loyalties to the point of frustration:

> *Feeling the aggression of the North, resenting their denial of the equal rights of our citizens to the common territory of the Commonwealth, etc., I am not pleased with the course of the "Cotton States," as they term themselves. In addition to their selfish, dictatorial bearing, the threats they throw out against the "Border States," as they call them, if they will not join them, argues little for the benefit or peace of Virginia, should she determine to coalesce with them. While I wish to do what is right, I am unwilling to do what is wrong at the bidding of the South or of the North.*

Lee's frustration, concern and growing pessimism about what lay ahead was further expressed in another letter written to his son Rooney in January 1861:

> *I can anticipate no greater calamity for the country than a dissolution of the Union. It would be an accumulation of all the evils we complain of, & I am willing to sacrifice every thing but honour for its preservation… Secession is nothing but revolution.*

Colonel Robert E. Lee, United States Army, would now have to make a decision that would alter the course of history. Lee had given most of his life to the Union for which his father, Henry Lee, the famous, "Light Horse Harry" Lee, had fought. Robert was born at the Lee ancestral mansion, Stratford Hall, and drew his first breath in the same room where two signers of the Declaration of Independence, Richard Henry Lee and Francis Lightfoot Lee, were born. Robert E. Lee had also married Mary Custis, daughter of George Washington Parke Custis, the adopted grandson of George Washington, and it is common knowledge that Lee idolized George Washington—America's near perfect model of the citizen-soldier. Lee was one of those Virginians who had an "inherited attachment to the Union," and his strong ties to the Union, and its founding, were by blood as well as by choice—and he was purposely conscious of both.

Given just these circumstances, it would be easy to understand the depth of Lee's love for, and loyalty to, the Union. But there was more. By the age of fifty-four, Colonel Robert E. Lee had fought with honor and distinction in the Mexican War, served as superintendent of West Point and quelled a domestic insurrection at Harpers Ferry. He was, by all accounts, the epitome of the nineteenth-century American soldier.

Thus, President Lincoln's offering the command of the Union forces to Lee was a wise decision. Not only was it the prevailing opinion that Lee was the most qualified to take command, but Lincoln also knew that if Lee accepted, his stature alone might bring a quicker end to the conflict. Lincoln, however, underestimated Lee's competing loyalties and loves: Virginia and his family. Lee expressed the sentiments of many in Lexington when he penned these now-famous words to his sister on April 20, 1861:

> *Now we are in a state of war which will yield to nothing. The whole South is in a state of revolution, into which Virginia, after a long struggle, has been drawn; and though I recognize no necessity for the state of things, and would have forborne and pleaded to the end for redress of grievances, real or supposed, yet in my own person I had to meet the question whether I should take part against my native State. With all my devotion to the Union, and the feeling of loyalty and duty of an American citizen, I have not been able to make up my mind to raise my hand against my relative, my children, my home. I have, therefore, resigned my commission in the Army, and save in defense of my native State (with the sincere hope that my poor services may never be needed) I hope I may never be called upon to draw my sword.*

Lee's competing loyalties would lead to the struggle of a lifetime. On April 18, 1861, after declining Lincoln's offer, Lee went immediately to General Scott's office in Washington and informed him of his decision. Lee's friend and comrade in arms responded with a statement Lee had not fully anticipated: "I feared it would be so…If you purpose to resign, it is proper that you should do so at once; your present attitude is equivocal."

Until now, Lee had remained hopeful that he would not be forced to resign from the army he loved unless and until Virginia seceded and its citizens affirmed the ordinance of secession. That hope was now dashed. Though Lee had declined the offer of command, he would not be able to deny service if he were called on for duty once hostilities commenced. Scott had made that painfully clear. At that point, Lee would have to "resign under orders. That was a disgrace to any soldier."

In fact, Virginia did pass an ordinance of secession on the afternoon of April 17 but had kept the news secret until Virginia militia units could seize Federal arsenals within its borders. Lee read the headlines two days later on the morning of April 19. With a sense of impending doom in the air, Lee rode home to Arlington. He would never again cross the Potomac as an officer in the United States Army. Lee's most famous biographer, Douglas Southall Freeman, pointed out that Lee's decision was difficult and suggests he may have had second thoughts:

> *But he did not leave his problem behind him as he turned his back on his country's capital. He carried it with him; he wrestled with it. Was his position equivocal? Ought he to resign at once, regardless of what Virginia did?...his own mind was so opposed to secession, and his devotion to the Union and to the army proved so strong, now it was put to the test.*

After supper at Arlington on April 19, Lee walked up the stairs to his room, where he would wrestle with God and his devotion to the Union. Downstairs, Lee's wife, Mary, heard him drop to his knees in prayer and then return to his feet, pacing back and forth. Did he think of his career? What about the Union and the republic his ancestors had such an important role in establishing? What would the future hold for his family? What would the future hold for his native Virginia, in whose soil lay his ancestors?

It is not unlikely that Robert E. Lee thought more than once that night of his father. Light Horse Harry Lee was a favorite of General Washington and was chosen by Congress to eulogize our first president. It was in his eulogy of Washington that Lee's father first coined the phrase: "First in war, first in peace, and first in the hearts of his countrymen." Did Lee recall some other words uttered by his father—words that now seemed to apply to his own life? During a debate in 1798 with James Madison, Lee's father had stated, "Virginia is my country; her will I obey, however lamentable the fate to which it may subject me."

Some twenty-first-century Americans might scoff at the thought of a state being viewed as a "country." With today's political realities, that scoffing might be warranted. But that was certainly not the case in 1861. It should be noted that at that time, Virginia had been a political entity for more than two hundred years, and Lee's roots in Virginia could be traced to the year 1640. The United States had been a reality for only about eighty years. Furthermore,

Military Institute superintendent Francis Smith also voiced pro-secession sentiments in a town meeting held when South Carolina's secession was the topic of discussion. Other VMI faculty, along with a number of prominent citizens, including church leaders and local politicians who were present at the meeting, uniformly criticized South Carolina. Smith is said to have risen and offered his "support and sympathy" for the Palmetto State. Many local townspeople were incensed and promptly charged Smith with "disloyalty and treachery." The backlash was so severe, historian Bradford Wineman points out, that "in March 1861, the state legislature denied a much needed appropriations bill for VMI because of the 'treasonable' comments Smith made." How dramatically would these positions soon change.

The citizens of Lexington and surrounding Rockbridge County were still divided on the question of secession during the winter of 1860–61. Nonetheless, Lexington had elected anti-secessionists to Virginia's Secession Convention in Richmond. Shenandoah Valley native and historian Robert Moore shares his insight on this topic.

SOUTHERN UNIONISM IN LEXINGTON AND ROCKBRIDGE COUNTY, VIRGINIA

By Robert Moore

The path that Robert E. Lee followed in making his decision on Virginia's secession differed little from that of Southern Unionists. The difference was where the respective courses changed and how those courses were altered by an individual and personal understanding of responsibilities and commitments. In many of those decisions, eventual actions can be defined as either conditional or unconditional Unionism. Lee's Unionism had its breaking point; it was conditional. Others did not; they were unconditional. The same could be said of those who committed to secession and the Confederacy. Some embraced it, seemingly without condition, while others went only as far as personal levels of tolerance would allow. There were still others who muddy our understanding even more, leaving us uncertain as to what inspired personal courses and guessing as to how many more categories might be necessary to define the waxing and waning of wartime sentiments.

In Lexington and Rockbridge County, devotion to the Union was genuine and, early on, unwavering among the majority. With the presidential election of 1860, only three districts—Natural Bridge, Collierstown and Dryden—demonstrated substantial interests in secession, and even they failed to put John C. Breckinridge ahead of the more moderate Constitutional Union candidate, John Bell. By carrying Bell in every district, the county demonstrated a desire for more peaceful solutions, as opposed to an immediate and reckless plunge toward secession. Part of what formed the foundation of this stand were three fundamental beliefs of the Constitutional Union party: "the constitution, the union, and the enforcement of laws."

Despite the unraveling of the Deep South, immediately following the election of Abraham Lincoln, cooler heads prevailed in Lexington and Rockbridge. The *Lexington Gazette*, a clear advocate for Union, maintained:

> *Now that he* [Lincoln] *has been elected, what can he do? The Conservative party have a majority in both houses of Congress. The Supreme Court is Conservative. The Executive can enforce no law prejudicial to the institution of slavery, if Congress enacts none. Every act he does is done under the solemn oath which he takes at his inauguration. Had we not then better try him? It may be that he will prove to be a conscientious and law-abiding man. Mr. Jefferson went the full length Lincoln goes against slavery. We have not had an ultra pro-slavery president, unless Mr. Tyler may be called so, and yet all the time the institution of slavery had been safe from executive interference.*

Still, concerns over an increasingly growing national crisis warranted discussion. As such, a committee of twelve was formed, on which some of the most prominent local citizens, many of them Lexingtonians, served, including T.J. Jackson, E.F. Paxton and others. In the wake of the formation, meetings were held and resolutions passed regarding public sentiment on the course of both the county and the commonwealth. Not unlike the "constitution, union, and enforcement of laws" mindset demonstrated in the presidential election, the same was sought in finding solutions in response to Southern grievances. Could the national crisis be averted without damaging the Union, and if so, how? At a meeting on December 15, 1860, "the leading grievances against the South were enumerated as the aggressive anti-slavery agitation in the North, the personal liberty bills [interfering with the capture of runaway slaves on free-state soil], and the appeals to the spirit of insurrection and murder" (as in the example of the John Brown Raid on Harpers Ferry). The timing is interesting considering, three days later, John J. Crittenden addressed these same grievances in his proposed "compromise"; this would meet with general approval in Lexington and Rockbridge County in the month to come, having been deemed "a just and honorable basis for settlement of our national difficulties." The "plan" to handle the grievances guaranteed slavery; the upholding of fugitive slave laws, even on free soil; and that the slave line of the Missouri Compromise be expanded. Crittenden's plan also prevented any appeal or amendments to the compromise.

These same meetings also reflected an overall concern, if not an outright disdain, for a course to secession. One resolution specified:

> *We cannot deem it the part of wise and brave Christian patriots even yet to despair the republic. We feel it to be a high duty as well as the dictate of true policy on the part of Virginia to struggle for the redress of her grievances within the Union.*

While declaring a promise for the preservation of the Union, another resolution did begin to outline the limits to which they would go for the Union—that it was "highly inexpedient in the present crisis to resort to coercion against any seceding state." In time, this would be a defining point in the decisions of many in the area, while the concerns for the future of slavery dominated the interests of others.

In the months to come, and with each cotton state's departure from the Union, support wavered among some, but the county seemed to retain its resolve. The ever-strong Unionist voice of the *Lexington Gazette*, not unlike the *Spectator* in nearby Staunton, showed particular alarm when talks of a Virginia Convention were raised, in that it would serve only to be "a piece of machinery that will be operated by secessionists to carry Virginia out of the Union." Further:

> *If we allow it to go down, we believe that with it will go down the last hope of civil and religious liberty. Let us not follow the example of South Carolina who seeks to put an unanswerable argument into the mouths of despots. South Carolina has said by her action that a republican government can be dissolved at any time, that it is a government without power, that it is no government at all.*

When the convention appeared to be a reality and it came time to seek delegates, moderates Samuel McDowell Moore and James Baldwin Dorman were the first to be nominated as potential representatives of Rockbridge County, followed by J.W. Brockenbrough and C.C. Baldwin. Though having supported Douglas in the 1860 election, Dorman had, in December, voiced his opinion against separation from the United States. Moore was also of the same line of thought. Brockenbrough and Baldwin, on the other hand, were more in the opposite pendulum swing—Brockenbrough believing that the "Union that the constitution gave us no longer exists" and Baldwin supporting immediate secession. On February 4, 1861, Dorman and Moore received 1,869 and 1,838 votes, respectively, easily defeating those with more hasty intentions.

In the nearly two and a half months that followed, the battle over Virginia's future was waged in Richmond. Alexander H.H. Stuart, from neighboring Augusta, noted:

> *The disunionists from all parts of the state have been here in force, and have sought to bring every influence to bear to precipitate Virginia into secession and civil war. Secession is a doctrine of New England origin. It is at war with the whole theory of our institutions, and is subversive of every principle of popular government. In my opinion, there is no natural antagonism between the Northern and the Southern states. They* [the sections] *are the complements of each other. The present alienation is the work of designing men. I believe that all our wrongs can be effectually redressed in the Union. Secession, instead of being a remedy, would be an aggravation. It would lead to emancipation, and probably to emancipation in blood. Should the Union be dissolved peaceably, the policy of the new government will be shaped by the cotton states. Free trade, and direct taxation for the support of the Federal government, will be the cardinal features of that policy. The expense of maintaining the present government of the United States, ranging from $60,000,000 to $100,000,000 a year, is raised by duties and is voluntarily paid in the form of increased prices by those who buy foreign goods. Under the other system, the tax would be involuntary, and Virginia's part would be about $5,000,000. This would be a very heavy burden. South Carolina's causes of dissatisfaction are financial and not the same as ours.*

Despite the efforts of secessionists, Unionist delegates, including Moore and Dorman of Rockbridge, attempted to keep secessionists in check. In one situation, Moore refused to give support to a proposal that would seemingly tie Virginia's fate, without distinction, to that of the cotton states. Oren Morton noted:

> *Mr. Moore…said the cotton states had not consulted Virginia, and he did not intend to be bound hand and foot by them. He would neither be hurried out of the Union, nor kept in it by precipitate action. If compelled to go anywhere, he was determined to know first where he was going, who he was to go with and what was to be his conduction after he did go.*

Moore did, however, echo warnings against coercion, and was "ready to resist sending troops through Virginia to attack the seceding states, but if the latter thought proper to attack any United States fort, they would have to abide the consequences."

Eventually, after considerable deliberation, the first call for a vote came on April 4, resulting in Dorman and Moore voting against secession. Following the bombardment of Fort Sumter and Lincoln's call for troops from Virginia, the convention was again brought to vote. While Lincoln's call for troops was enough to convince many, the final determining factor in pushing the majority of the rest across may have been in ex-governor Henry Wise's announcement that Virginia troops were already moving to seize Harpers Ferry. In the vote on that day, April 17, the Rockbridge delegates switched in favor of secession.

Even in Lexington, the atmosphere must have felt thick. Despite word arriving on April 16 that Fort Sumter had been fired upon, those who continued to hold on to Unionists sentiments also appeared to hold their ground. Only after a rather heated episode over flags, flagpoles and hot-tempered cadets, and into the next day, when official word was given that President Lincoln had called for troops, did the general spirit seem to shift in earnest.

As had been made clear a few months before, coercion would bring about quicker resolve by Virginia, and therefore the county, and this marked for many an attitude of conditional Unionism. Even among the more cool-headed delegates, sentiments shifted. In a letter to a cousin, Dorman wrote, on April 16, of "Lincoln's arrogant and infamous usurpation of power."

As people with such a mind began to mobilize for war, others resolved that the final decision had not yet been made. The referendum on secession, for example, would not come for more than a month.

Within that interim, those who did not commit with some degree of determination in favor of Virginia's course into the Confederacy faced myriad woes, and those who continued to remain outspoken on Unionism stood to suffer even more. Unlike before, being outspoken on Unionism now came as one teetering dangerously on the edge of what the new majority felt qualified as another form of treason—or at the very least, something dangerous to the objectives of the new majority. Even so, some, such as Governor John Letcher's uncle William Davidson, continued to be vocal in their positions on Unionism. Reconstruction-appointed Lexington postmaster J.H. Freeman recalled that Davidson was a "very plain and outspoken friend of the Union. Made himself unpopular by his advocacy of the Union Cause. I heard a number of persons say that if he hadn't been the uncle of Gov. Letcher he would have been hung."

James Lam, of Whistle Creek, was also seen as one who dangerously voiced his sentiments. Testifying on his behalf, James Harrison recalled:

> *I remember one occasion when a secessionist made a speech in Lexington, in the court-house…after it was over I went around the corner of the clerk's office and saw the claimant standing there talking to some other person, I said to him that he ought to have been in, and heard the speech and he just remarked, "God damn the speech."*

John Lam was threatened merely for his being known as a Unionist:

> *E.S. Tutwiler, Wm. Bumpers, Baxter McCorkle, here on the streets of Lexington, threatened to shoot me and had his pistol out, and perhaps would have shot me, had I opened my mouth, just because I was a union man.*

While Brownsburg's Mary Potter was not threatened, she remembered differently her husband's circumstances. "I was never threatened. But my husband was. He was threatened with being hung by persons in the village near by."

When it did come time for the referendum, the *Lexington Gazette* warned:

> *The tarring, etc., of those voters who are against the ordinance of secession* [is] *subversive of law and order. If a free citizen is not to be allowed to exercise his free will in casting his vote, then the submission of the question is mere mockery.*

When May 23 finally arrived, intimidation appeared to impact many of those who had not embraced secession following Lincoln's call for troops. People such as John Lam and Philip Engleman didn't vote against it as they felt doing so was not safe. Others who later claimed to be loyal, such as James G. Dixon, recalled that, at that point, "we were into the war and I thought it best to vote for the ordinance of secession."

Leroy C. Gilbert, of Fancy Hall, decided not to vote at all: "I neither voted for or against the ordinance of secession. I held to the stars and stripes during the whole war."

But what was at the root of such loyalty? Documented words of Unionists from Lexington and Rockbridge County can best be found in Southern Loyalist Claims applications and, generally, are uncomplicated voices of demonstration that reveal simple personal perspectives on what they perceived as responsible and patriotic citizens of the Republic. "I wanted no other Government than the old U.S. Govt.," noted Andrew Shaver in his claim. "I desired to see the Government placed in the same condition as it was before the war. I was truly glad when the war ended as it did. My sympathies were with the Govt. under which I was raised."

William Davidson specified both treason and slavery as the root reasons for his opposition to secession and the Confederacy. In testifying on behalf of Davidson, Dr. J.H. Freeman noted:

> *I frequently talked with him about the war more than any other man in the county. He said that it was a Negro holder's war and that slavery was dead when the first gun was fired at Fort Sumter. He was opposed to the war and said that the leaders of the Confederacy were a set of traitors. He said the Confederacy would fail and ought to fail.*

Davidson, as Freeman pointed out, was also a veteran of the War of 1812 and knew Davidson "would have suffered his right arm to have been taken off sooner than have voted for the ordinance of secession. He would not recognize the Confederate government at all."

Even after the referendum, Rockbridge's remaining Unionists were still required to tread lightly. Eli Swartz said of Gilbert, "I heard Capt. McClintock say that he ought to be watched, that he was a dangerous man to the South." In fact, Gilbert himself recalled that he was "threatened to be taken to Castle Thunder because I talked too much in favor of the United States."

Unionism was often seen as part of a war within a war but also involved yet another tier of war, which divided nuclear families and challenged Unionists' basic need to act in the best manner possible to ensure survival of self and, eventually, the reunification of families, despite temporary differences. Most of Rockbridge's claimants had sons and brothers who were in the ranks of the Confederate army. Some fathers claimed, despite the enlistment of sons against the will of their fathers, that they still provided for the boys as if they were part of the family. No matter what, such gestures often ensured the failure of a claims application.

Though not seen often in Rockbridge County's story, something that tested Unionists even more so in the valley was the very Union force that the Unionists wished to see successful. When General David Hunter moved on Lexington, John Lam indicated that his home was visited, and despite having been identified as a Unionist by a local black guide, the Union forces still needed his stock for the army. George Adams recalled of Lam's plight:

> *When near Lexington, just in the edge of the field, one of the private soldiers shot one of the cattle and the claimant said, "There they have killed one of my cattle now" and also that he was a union man and they ought not to take his cattle, then the soldiers who had shot one of the cattle spoke up and said, "Damn you, if you are a union man support the union."*

It's likely that such incidents tried Unionists to what later became their breaking point, where even they found a need to define themselves as conditional Unionists. Others, however, continued to undermine the Confederacy. Many, such as James Lam and Mary Potter, harbored and fed Confederate deserters. "I fed deserters from the Rebel army," remembered Potter, "and some of the Union soldiers passing with Genl. Crook and Gen. Hunter's Army." Other Unionists took even greater strides to circumvent the effectiveness of the Confederate cause.

Without doubt, those from the county who opted to wear blue were rare, but there were those who might be considered more absolute and demonstrative in their Unionism. The ability to find a number that might be even close to accurate will require years of careful combing through both Union pension records and service records of all the Union forces in search of birthplaces and particulars that better detail the decision to join the U.S. military. In the meantime, a cursory review of the 1890 Veterans' Schedule for Rockbridge provides only a few names of those who might have been locals and even fewer who were local without a doubt. James Lowman, of Buffalo, for example, was one man who took such steps, enlisting with the Third West Virginia Cavalry in 1864.

While we can see various examples of words and actions taken by Unionists, there are still questions that remain about others. What of that which might be interpreted as indecisiveness and reluctance? Was such a thing indicative of possible Unionists sentiments, or were they simply matters of people wishing to be left alone?

In the spring of 1862, for example, with the coming of the first Confederate conscription, in addition to the 385 who had been judged physically disqualified and the 96 who had been exempted because of duties such as miller, overseer and blacksmith, 93 refused service outright. Were they Unionists, or did they prefer to remain out altogether?

Even as far along as the days before the Second Battle of Manassas, the local newspaper remarked on how it was apparent that many in the county had not yet committed themselves: "If every part of the Confederacy has as many idle young men in it as this quiet little town of Lexington, we might raise a splendid army in addition to the forces now in the field."

In April 1864, evidence of disillusionment and reluctance was considered by the local newspaper when it claimed that citizens had been evading impressment of supplies. In light of the lack of enthusiasm, it was found necessary to call on local civilian law, such as "the sheriff, or any constable, and such official…to summon any number of citizens to take impressed articles by force. A refusal to do so will be in contempt of court." Whether inspired by Unionists sentiments, examples do reveal less than total commitment to the hopes held by the Southern Confederacy.

Overall, during the period after Lincoln's call for troops, Rockbridge County offers challenges to those who go looking for accurate measures of Unionism. Unlike in most of the valley counties, Southern Claims applications were low, numbering fewer than twenty-five, with only one approved. Even so, assessing Lexington's and Rockbridge County's Unionism based merely on the number of applications alone would be a mistake. Rockbridge was not, as most counties in the central and lower valley, a place where Union troops were frequently marching through or remained for enough time to create a demand on the supplies of local civilians. Furthermore, though only one claim was approved, this is more a reflection of the Claims Commission than of the applicants themselves. The commission was highly critical and disallowed and barred applications that, to a researcher today, seem to be poor assessments of Unionism. To be sure, Unionism was present in Rockbridge but seems less prevalent than what would be found in many of the rest of the counties of the valley.

The opposing sentiments represented by those who were of Lee's mindset versus those who wished to remain loyal to the Union would manifest themselves in very dramatic ways at two of the town's most prominent institutions.

given off just enough light for the conspirators to see that one misstep would mean certain death.

The flag was secured to the Rotunda's lightning rod—a symbolically fitting support—and brought to life by the winds "just as the first faint streaks of dawn appeared on the eastern hills." As the news spread through the halls of the university, law professor John B. Minor made known his disapproval as he walked to his lecture room by reciting an impromptu verse of rhyme: "Flag of my country, can it be; That rag's up there instead of thee!"

As one student after another scaled the steps of the Rotunda to exhort the crowd for the Southern cause, the growing multitude became more and more boisterous. Then the stout form of mathematics professor Albert Taylor Bledsoe appeared. There was immediate silence. Bledsoe climbed to the top of the Rotunda steps. While Professor Minor was a staunch Unionist, Bledsoe had made his Southern sympathies well known, interspersing his calculus lectures with what McKim called "vigorous remarks in the doctrine of States' rights." Looking out over the excited assembly, the wise Bledsoe sought to defuse the situation without dampening the spirit—with which he agreed in principle. He assured his listeners that he was confident that the boys who had placed the flag atop the Rotunda were "the very nicest fellows in the University."

Bledsoe reasoned, however, that since Virginia had not yet voted to secede, flying the "secession flag" was not the proper thing to do at that time. He advised the young men to take down the flag but added in a sympathetic tone, "Young gentlemen, do it very tenderly." McKim would go on to serve in the Confederate army, first as a private, then as a staff officer and finally as a chaplain. Bledsoe would serve the Confederacy as a colonel and later became acting assistant secretary of war.

This act of rebellion was not the first, nor the only, of its kind on a Virginia college campus, as the commonwealth was now in the thick of debating secession. As historian Peter Carmichael noted in his book *The Last Generation: Young Virginians in Peace, War, and Reunion*, the raising of secession flags after the election of Abraham Lincoln became somewhat commonplace:

> *At each of these demonstrations, Virginia students raised secession flags to symbolize their bold and unequivocal stand for Southern Independence. The highly politicized rituals also marked a declaration of independence from adult authority and influence...Discarding the Stars and Stripes for secessionist banners, therefore, was not a careless gesture; it was a calculated political act that reflected a profound shift in allegiance from*

> *the United States to the South...In the month that preceded the firing on Fort Sumter on April 12, students raised secession flags at William and Mary, the Virginia Military Institute, Roanoke College, and Lynchburg College. Evidence suggests that young people at Emory and Henry, Randolph-Macon, and Hampden-Sydney also agitated for disunion.*

But the distinction of being the first body of students to raise the flag of secession over a Virginia college campus belongs to the students of Washington College in Lexington. The first incident at the school occurred in the later part of December 1860. Though it was the first in Virginia, and at the school, it would not be the last at Washington College. Though the flag-raising at the University of Virginia appeared to be little more than a student prank, across the Blue Ridge Mountains in the Shenandoah Valley to the west, these types of student protests would be much more confrontational. Peter Carmichael notes the following:

> *The students at Washington College became the first to unfurl a secessionist flag in a surreptitious ceremony that occurred in late December 1860. Although far ahead of their peers, the actions of Washington College students reveal the generational dynamic of flag-raising ceremonies as declarations against both Unionism and adult authority...Numerous flag raisings revealed that Virginia campuses were the epicenter of secessionism, and the tremors that emanated from the ivory towers shook young people into action across the state.*

In an article titled "Stonewall Jackson's Scabbard Speech," which appears in volume 16 of the *Southern Society Historical Papers*, William A. Obenchain made this observation regarding the "generational dynamic" to which Carmichael refers:

> *In the town of Lexington there were many "conditional" Union men and some unconditional Secessionists. But Secession had then its strongest and rashest advocates amongst the students of Washington College...Whenever the seeds of revolution are floating in the political atmosphere, they generally find in the colleges and universities their most congenial soil. Lexington proved no exception to the rule.*

Nowhere did this dynamic manifest itself so publicly and so early in the conflict as it did at Washington College in Lexington. So strong was the secession sentiment among Washington College students that it quickly led to the resignation of the school's well-respected seventy-year-old president, the Reverend George Junkin. Junkin was born and raised in Pennsylvania and became president of the school in 1848. An ordained Presbyterian minister, Junkin was also a staunch Unionist. Ironically, Junkin was close to Thomas (Stonewall) Jackson and was Jackson's father-in-law from Jackson's first marriage. Though Junkin would forever "loathe all things secessionist," his affection for Jackson would remain steadfast.

Reverend George Junkin. *Special Collections, Leyburn Library, Washington and Lee University.*

After Junkin resigned, he returned to his home in Pennsylvania, where he lived out the remainder of his days, dying at his son's home in Philadelphia in 1868. After he left Virginia, Junkin penned an article, first published in the *Presbyterian Standard*, detailing his version of the events that led to his resigning the presidency of Washington College. The article then appeared in numerous papers throughout the North. The article also appeared in a book Junkin authored titled *Political Fallacies*. The article begins with Junkin describing an "exposition to the Senior Class in Washington College" in which he articulated his views of the Constitution in regards to federalism and states' rights. The exposition may have been a response to what Junkin witnessed at the school's weekly oratorical exercises, held every Friday afternoon. Historian W.G. Bean has written in his book *The Liberty Hall Volunteers: Stonewall's College Boys* that "the students often selected for their orations recent speeches of Southern Congressmen in defense of secession." Junkin considered such views treason and was often visibly upset, ordering these students to "sit down, sir." He concluded the summation of his exposition with these words: "The pseudo right of secession is a national wrong."

This did not sit well with the pro-Southern students at Washington College. Junkin recalled what happened as a result of his pro-Union stance:

> *But in the progress of these discussions I observed a growing restiveness among the students, heard myself called a "Pennsylvania Abolitionist" and saw written on the column opposite my recitation-room door, "Lincoln Junkin."*

Junkin then provides some details surrounding the placement of a "Palmetto flag" on the center building of the college:

> *In this process, led by a Georgia student, the copper lightning rod was bent, and subsequently broken off. For a student to go out on the roof has always been an offense, punished by demerit. This flag I ordered the servants to take down and bring to me. I was asked what I would do with it, and replied, "Burn it after evening prayer." But whilst I was at dinner, they procured a ladder, climbed into the window of my lecture-room, and took the flag away. About a week after, it was again erected. I immediately ordered the servants to take it down, and at an hour when all except the Freshmen were at their recitations; these stood about as spectators, and asked what I was going to do with it. I answered, "I'll show you." I ordered the servants to hold the butt of the flag-pole firmly, and throw the top over from the chapel roof, which is a story lower than the centre building. When the flag came within reach, I stepped up and took some matches out of my pocket, set it on fire, and, when it blazed up, told the servants to throw the pole out from the building, and whilst it flamed up, I said, "So perish all efforts to dissolve this glorious Union."*

Junkin then makes special effort to footnote what he believed to be the prophetic outcome of his warning:

> *It is worthy of special notice here, that the young men who were chiefly active in the erecting of these flags perished on July 21, 1861, in the first battle of Bull Run. Two of them were killed by one cannon-shot, and a third (and he the leader) perished from excessive over-exertion in carrying his wounded companion three miles to the railroad car. This companion breathed his last just as they were lifting him on the car. And thus, to a melancholy and fearful extent, has the malediction prophetic been accomplished. I am to this day—Dec. 9, 1862—but very imperfectly informed on the subject, by reason of the rebellion cutting off all intercourse between me and my two sons and daughter in Rockbridge; but, from all I have heard, I am painfully impressed with*

> *the belief that more than fifty per cent, of all those misguided youth who were active in rebelling against me have paid the forfeit of their folly by the sacrifice of their lives. This is cause of unfeigned sorrow; for a very large proportion of them were youth of remarkable promise for talents, diligence in study, purity of moral and religious character; who, but for these bloody fallacies, would have lived long and adorned the higher walks of professional life.*

But Junkin's burning of the secessionist flag only emboldened the Washington College students. Junkin details the escalation of the now full-throated rebellion:

> *On the 15th of April, my lecture-room door was much injured by attempts to break it open with a strong iron bar. The library door they succeeded in forcing open. The object was to procure the jointed ladder, which the servants had put behind the amphitheatre for safe keeping. (A door opens between the library-room and my lecture-room.) On the morning of the 17th, I saw a disunion flag surmounting the statue of Washington and the lightning-rod.*

Peter Carmichael writes that Junkin had become so outraged over the student body ignoring his orders that he "conducted a thorough inspection of the college, charging unannounced into students' rooms and 'squealing' for the flag he never located." Finally, Junkin had had enough. He would either put down this rebellion, or he would withdraw from the institution he had so faithfully served and loved for over twelve years. Junkin writes what happened after the day's prayer:

> *I detained the members of the Faculty, and waved my hand to the students to retire. I stated to my colleagues that this thing must be stopped, etc. One of them said he had just received a petition on the subject, signed by most of the students. I asked him to read it. The substance (I have not a copy) of it was, that the flag which they had erected might be permitted to remain. I stated to the Faculty that it had been placed there in violation of law, and in contemptuous resistance to my express order, and, of course, if they would grant the prayer of the petition, my course of duty was clear and plain—I could not be coerced, but would instantly secede; and left them to deliberate, and let me know their decision.*

It is interesting that Junkin apparently found no irony in using the term "secede" in his threat to separate from the college over its pro-secession sentiments. Things continued to deteriorate:

> *At eleven o'clock, the usual hour, the Junior class came into my room. I asked whether the flag was on the top of the College, and received an affirmative answer. "Then, gentlemen," said I, "I am under the necessity of assuring you that I cannot submit to this kind of coercion," and dismissed them. One rushed toward the door, shouting, "Thank God for that! I thank God for that!" and yelled his utmost, in which he was joined by a few others.*

Junkin had clearly lost control of the situation. After confronting the juniors, Junkin then addressed the seniors over the flag issue and the disregard for his orders:

> *At twelve o'clock, when the Seniors came in, I read to them the substance of what I had said to the Juniors, and which, meanwhile, to be sure of the identical words, I had written down as follows: "Is the flag still on the top of the College?" Answer, "Yes." "Well, then, gentlemen, as you put it there in express opposition to my order, I am under the necessity of telling you that I have never been ridden over rough-shod in that style, and I never will be; therefore, I never will hear a recitation or deliver a lecture under a rebel flag. The class is dismissed.*

Nonetheless, the older, more mature seniors exhibited more respect for Reverend Junkin than did the junior class, with Junkin noting that "they rose and withdrew in the most gentlemanly and respectful manner, with every appearance of sincere regret."

But it mattered little. Junkin was, by now, clearly in the minority, and the students had allies among the faculty as well as the trustees of the school. The tide of secession sentiment had washed ashore and would not be abated. That same day, Junkin received the following communication from the faculty of Washington College:

> *W. College, April 17, 1861.*
> *Action of the Faculty in relation to the Flag on the College Buildings.*
>
> *Whereas, The students, in reference to the tidings that the Virginia Convention are about to adopt an ordinance of secession, have hoisted a*

Southern flag upon the college building, and have made a respectful request of the Faculty that they would permit it to remain; and whereas, the Faculty have assurance that this act has not taken place in any desire to violate college laws, or offer indignity to any member of the Faculty—an assurance given by the students themselves to a member of the Faculty, and confirmed by the fact that they promptly took down, at the request of the Faculty, a similar flag, erected on a former occasion; and whereas, Dr. Junkin regards this act as a willful violation of law and a personal indignity, and requires the Faculty to have it removed at once, on penalty of his resignation—an alternative which the Faculty think that Dr. Junkin has no right to impose, and which we cannot allow to influence our action in the premises, although we are fully determined to sustain the president, or any individual member of our body, in the maintenance of discipline; and whereas, the sole object of the Faculty is to allay excitement, and insure good order and attention to study in college, in this time of civil disturbance, believing, as we do, that these ends will be best promoted by not requiring the immediate removal of the flag; therefore, Resolved, That the flag be permitted to remain, at the discretion of the Faculty. Copied from the minutes, and communicated to Dr. Junkin by order of the Faculty.
J.L. Campbell, Clerk

The following afternoon, Junkin called a meeting of the trustees and tendered his simply worded resignation:

Washington College, April 18, A.D. 1861.
To the Board of Trustees of Washington College.

Gentlemen,—I hereby resign the office to which you called me more than twelve years ago.

Very respectfully,
Your humble servant,
Geo. Junkin, President.

Junkin then notes that "the vote was passed, I shook hands with all the members, many of whom, as well as myself, were overpowered with tender emotions." The faculty, upon hearing of Junkin's resignation, then wrote him a conciliatory note:

Washington College, April 18, 1861.
Rev. Geo. Junkin, D.D.

Dear Sir,—Although we, your recent colleagues, as members of the Faculty of Washington College, felt it to be our duty, under peculiar circumstances, to pursue a line of policy which you did not approve, and in consequence of which you have felt constrained to resign your connection with the Institution, we wish to say, that we were actuated by no feelings of disrespect to you personally, or disregard of the high position you have filled in the College for so many years. And we desire now to express our high regard for your manly virtues as a Christian minister, and as a gentleman of distinguished talents and learning; and to assure you of our entire confidence in your integrity, of our sincere friendly regards for yourself and family, and our earnest prayer, that the twilight of your life may be its brightest and happiest period.
With much esteem, we are, very sincerely,
Your friends, J.L. Campbell, A.L. Nelson, James J. White, C.J. Harris

Having severed his ties with Washington College and, no doubt, feeling dejected, Junkin was in no mood to stay in Lexington long. The very next day, Junkin, "set to work in winding up my business, selling my property, paying my debts, etc., and, as the ways of public conveyance were then blocked, I purchased a carriage, drove my own horses three hundred and fifty miles to Oxford, Chester County."

Several sources claim that when Junkin arrived at the Mason-Dixon line, he disembarked from his carriage and ceremoniously wiped the Southern mud from his boots, symbolically ridding himself of any vestige of the rebellious South and making sure he was not guilty of carrying Rebel dirt into the Union.

Thus, Lexington had seen—figuratively speaking—its first casualty of the Civil War, all stemming from the "rebellious" Washington College students. But many of these same students who were so quick to call for war would also fall as casualties. Those casualties would be literal.

A secessionist flag was not the only thing being raised at Washington College in the spring of 1861. A military unit was also in the making—one that would become part of Stonewall Jackson's legendary Stonewall Brigade. Even before Junkin had resigned, some Washington College students had petitioned faculty members for permission to form "a military class." The request was denied—initially. Evidently, since it occurred during the same time of the Junkin controversy, the faculty did not want to agitate the

John Letcher. *Special Collections, Leyburn Library, Washington and Lee University.*

situation any further. Despite this first rejection, a week later, the students again requested permission to organize a military company for preparation of what many saw as inevitable. This time, the faculty relented—but with certain terms. Anyone commanding the unit had to meet the approval of the faculty, no firearms could be possessed on campus grounds, no drills could take place during normal classroom hours and faculty could intervene at any time if they felt the activities were interfering with the normal function of the college. Initially, the "Liberty Hall Volunteers" did little more than "play military." But before school was over in early June, the nature of the drilling and campus atmosphere had taken on a much more serious tone. Young men who had no connection with Washington College began joining the ranks, and the grounds of the college took on the appearance of a full-fledged military camp. W.G. Bean noted, "Cadet W.H. Morgan of V.M.I. took over and soon had the company in a high state of proficiency."

On June 2, the boys of Washington College received orders from Virginia governor John Letcher to report immediately to Harpers Ferry. The bugle sounded loud and clear on the bright morning of June 8, and the company was readied for the march. The company of optimistic youths marched dutifully to the courthouse, where a crowd had gathered. There they were given a magnificent flag that had been hand-stitched by the devout ladies of the Falling Springs Presbyterian Church. Upon the flag was emblazoned the immortal Latin phrase *Pro Aris et Focis*—the English translation being simply "For Altar and Home."

As many of those young men read that Latin phrase, knowing full well what it meant, they truly believed that this represented what they were fighting for: their firesides, their native sod and their sacred places of worship. As the pastor of Falling Springs presented the flag to them with a fitting exhortation, these soon-to-be warriors were baptized with a benediction of fervent prayer by the Reverend William S. White, and tearful goodbyes were exchanged. W.G. Bean described the scene:

Headstone of William S. White, Stonewall Jackson Memorial Cemetery, Lexington, Virginia. *Photo by author.*

> *You could almost hear the heart-strings of mothers and sisters snap as they pressed sons and brothers in farewell embraces. In surrendering their boys to the services of Virginia, they were making sacrifices, such as their heroic ancestors were accustomed to make on the hills and among the mosshags of Scotland, for God and Presbytery. It was a willing sacrifice.*

After the emotional send-off, the friends and relatives of the boys returned to Falling Springs Presbyterian Church and petitioned God for their safety and their victory. On June 13, 1861, the *Lexington Gazette* described the unit as

> *one of the finest looking bodies of young soldiers that have been sent from this portion of the state…The patriotic fire which animated the breasts of the boys of Liberty Hall in the days of our Revolutionary struggle is still alive in the hearts of their worthy descendants.*

Among these new soldiers was Hugh Augustus White, younger brother of the commander James J. White and another son of Stonewall Jackson's pastor, William S. White. Hugh White had graduated from Washington

Above, left: James J. White, circa 1866–67. *Special Collections, Leyburn Library, Washington and Lee University.*

Above, right: Hugh A. White, circa 1858. *Special Collections, Leyburn Library, Washington and Lee University.*

College, but by the time Virginia seceded, he was a student at Union Theological Seminary in Farmville, Virginia. After a day of fasting and prayer at the seminary, Hugh wrote to his father on April 22, 1861:

> *We of Virginia are between two fires. If we join the one party, we join friends and allies; if we join the other, we join enemies and become vassals. Our decision then is formed, and we will seek to break the oppressor's yoke. Our only hope, under God, is in a united resistance even unto death...How delightful it would be to enter at once upon the work of saving men's souls, rather than in efforts to destroy their bodies.*

William White implored his son to complete his seminary studies rather than fight for the Confederacy, but the youthful patriot replied, "I have thought and prayed much over this question for two months...and the result is as firm a conviction that I ought at once to take part in the defense of my state...as I ever felt that I ought to preach the Gospel." His father could only respond, "Go, my son, and the blessing of God go with you."

Before the war, Hugh White had taught in one of Thomas J. "Stonewall" Jackson's Sunday school classes at the Lexington Presbyterian Church. During the war, he continued sharing his faith with other soldiers and was responsible for the conversion of at least one of his companions, Ted Barclay, who, after having a conversation with White, made a public profession of faith in Christ.

Headstone of Hugh A. White. *Photo by author.*

Barclay would write home of this experience: "I have had a conversation with Hugh White on the subject of religion and trust that I have found the way to heaven. I am willing to trust myself in the arms of the Saviour." It was Hugh White, however, who would soon be in the arms of his Savior, as he was killed at the Battle of Second Manassas and, according to General Jackson, "fell, sword in hand, gallantly cheering on his men."

Lexington Presbyterian Church, present day. *Photo by author.*

These young men proved that they were, indeed, "worthy descendants." Records indicate that of the original company, not a single soldier was ever discharged or otherwise punished for personal misconduct. As already noted, Company I, Fourth Virginia, the "Liberty Hall Volunteers," was composed primarily of students from Washington College. All the officers, as well as more than half the privates, were professing Christians, and one-fourth were candidates for the ministry.

Of course, there was another school that proved to be a hotbed of secessionist sentiment as well, and that also supplied numerous young men to fight for the Confederacy. Virginia Military Institute neighbors Washington College yet the two schools reflect, even to this day, great contrasts. In 1861, as many of the students at Washington College were preparing for the ministry and further theological study, the students at VMI were preparing to become "citizen-soldiers" and for war. The faculty and students at VMI were—more so than at any other school in the United States—keenly aware of the friction and divisions that were slowly but surely pushing the nation toward sectional conflict. After abolitionist John Brown was captured and sentenced to hang for leading an armed raid on the federal arsenal at Harpers Ferry, VMI's superintendent, Francis H. Smith, offered Virginia governor Henry A. Wise the services of VMI's Corps of Cadets to serve as additional security for Brown's execution at Charles Town, Virginia:

> *Va. Mil. Institute. Nov. 19th 1859*
> *His Excellency, H.A. Wise*
> *Richmond*
> *Dear Sir—*
> *The Adjutant General has shown me your communication to him dated Nov. 17th with reference to the propriety & expediency of ordering a detachment of the Corps of Cadets to be present at the execution of Brown & the others. When I originally tendered to your excellency the services of the Corps of Cadets for any duty which their military education might qualify them in the emergency now pressing upon the state, it was from the conviction that in all the essential elements of military defense they were better prepared than any other portion of the military of the state. More than this, I believe that the sentiment of any parent would respond to this patriotic duty on behalf of the sons, in giving protection to their own homes & firesides from the wicked assaults of incendiary & midnight marauders. My opinion in the prospect of their services being required now is unchanged. I can readily select 80 able bodied & well disciplined cadets acquainted with the Artillery drill, who will be ready to obey your excellency's order for the duty now claiming their service & I tender you my own services & those of Maj. Gilham & any other officer for duty in connection. Thanking you for this confidence that* [is] *placed in this Institution.*

As a plot by other abolitionists to help Brown escape from custody had already been discovered in October, Wise gladly accepted Smith's offer.

John Brown. *Library of Congress.*

John Brown depicted riding on his coffin to his execution. Wood engraving by Arthur Berghaus. *Library of Congress.*

The security detail consisted of two infantry companies of sixty-four cadets. Faculty member William Gilham was given overall command. In addition to the infantry companies, future Confederate general Major Thomas J. Jackson was placed in command of an artillery unit consisting of two howitzers manned by an additional twenty-one cadets. Also present was Major John Thomas Lewis Preston—Jackson's brother-in-law by Jackson's first marriage and professor of Latin at VMI. Preston's personal—and rather colorful—account of Brown's hanging describes in great detail what the VMI cadets would have witnessed on that December day:

> *Charles Town, Dec. 2, 1859*
> *The execution is over; we have just returned from the field and I sit down to give you some account of it. The weather was very favorable: the sky was*

Hunting party. *Left to right, standing*: George Washington Shields, Company I, Fourth Virginia Infantry; James Madison Pettigrew, Company I, Fourth Virginia Infantry; Rufus Barton McCrum, First Rockbridge Artillery; and Dudle McDowell (not a veteran). *Seated*: Joseph White, Lexington Home Guards; Colonel John Thomas Lewis Preston, Ninth Virginia Infantry and VMI; John W. Haughawout, Rockbridge Rangers and Senior Reserves; and John A. Preston (not a veteran). Circa 1865. *VMI Archives.*

Execution of John Brown depicted by C.L. McClung. *VMI Archives.*

a little overcast, with a gentle haze in the atmosphere that softened without obscuring the magnificent prospect afforded here.

Between eight and nine o'clock, the troops began to put themselves in motion to occupy the positions assigned to them on the field, as designated on the plan I send you. Col. Smith had been assigned the superintendence of the execution, and he and his staff were the only mounted officers on the ground, until the Major-General and his staff appeared. By ten o'clock all was arranged. The general effect was most imposing, and, at the same time, picturesque.

The cadets were immediately in rear of the gallows with a howitzer on the right and left, a little behind, so as to sweep the field. They were uniformed in red flannel shirts, which gave them a gay, dashing, Zouave look, and was exceedingly becoming, especially at the Battery. They were flanked obliquely by two corps, the Richmond Grays (Greys) and Company F, which if inferior in appearance to the cadets, were superior to any other company I ever saw outside of the regular army. Other companies were distributed over the field, amounting in all to about 800 men. The military force was about 1,500.

The whole enclosure was lined by cavalry troops posted as sentinels, with their officers—one on a peerless black horse, and another on a remarkable-looking white horse, continually dashing round the enclosure. Outside this enclosure were other companies acting as rangers and scouts. The jail was guarded by several companies of infantry, and pieces of artillery were put in position for its defense.

Shortly before eleven o'clock the prisoner was taken from the jail, and the funeral cortege was put in motion. First came three companies, then the criminal's wagon, drawn by two large white horses. John Brown was seated on his coffin, accompanied by the sheriff and two other persons. The wagon drove to the foot of the gallows, and Brown descended with alacrity and without assistance, and ascended the steep steps to the platform. His demeanor was intrepid, without being braggart. He made no speech; whether he desired to make one or not, I do not know. Had he desired it, it would not have been permitted. Any speech of his must, of necessity, have been unlawful, and as being directed against the peace and dignity of the Commonwealth, and as such could not be allowed by those who were then engaged in the most solemn and extreme vindication of law.

His manner was without trepidation, but his countenance was not free from concern, and it seemed to me to have a little cast of wildness. He stood upon the scaffold but a short time, giving brief adieus to those about him, when he was properly pinioned, the white cap drawn over his face, the noose adjusted and attached to the hook above, and he was moved blindfold a few steps forward. It was curious to note how the instincts of nature operated to make him careful in putting his feet as if afraid he would walk off the scaffold. The man who stood unblanched on the brink of eternity was afraid of falling a few feet to the ground.

He was now all ready. The sheriff asked him if he should give him a private signal before the fatal moment. He replied in a voice that seemed to me unnaturally natural, so composed was its tone, and so distinct its articulation, that "it did not matter to him, if only they would not keep him too long waiting." He was kept waiting, however. The troops that had formed his escort had to be put into their position, and while this was going on, he stood for some ten or fifteen minutes blindfold, the rope around his neck, and his feet on the treacherous platform, expecting instantly the fatal act. But he stood for this comparatively long time upright as a soldier in position, and motionless.

I was close to him, and watched him narrowly, to see if I could perceive any signs of shrinking or trembling in his person, but there was none. Once I thought I saw his knees tremble, but it was only the wind blowing his loose trousers. His firmness was subjected to still further trial by hearing Colonel Smith announce to the sheriff, "We are all ready, Mr. Campbell." The sheriff did not hear, or did not comprehend; and in a louder tone the same announcement was made. But the culprit still stood ready until the sheriff, descending the flight of steps, with a well-directed blow of a sharp hatchet, severed the rope that held up the trap door, which instantly sank beneath him, and he fell about three feet; and the man of strong and bloody hand, of fierce passions, of iron will, of wonderful vicissitudes, the terrible partisan of Kansas, the capturer of the United States Arsenal at Harpers Ferry, the would-be Catiline of the South, the demi-god of the abolitionists, the man execrated and lauded, damned and prayed for, the man who in his motives, his means, his plans, and his successes, must ever be a wonder, a puzzle, and a mystery—John Brown—was hanging between heaven and earth.

There was profound stillness during the time his struggles continued, growing feebler and feebler at each abortive attempt to breathe. He knees were scarcely bent, his arms were drawn up to a right angle at the elbow, with the hands clenched; but there was no writhing of the body, no violent heaving of the chest. At each feebler effort at respiration his arms sank lower, and his legs hung more relaxed, until at last, straight and lank he dangled, swayed to and fro by the wind.

It was a moment of deep solemnity, and suggestive of thoughts that make the bosom swell. The field of execution was a rising ground, and commanded the outstretching valley from mountain to mountain, and their still grandeur gave sublimity to the outline, while it so chanced that white clouds resting upon them, gave them the appearance that reminded more than one of us of the snow peaks of the Alps. Before us was the greatest array of disciplined forces ever seen in Virginia; infantry, cavalry and artillery combined, composed of the old Commonwealth's noblest sons, and commanded by her best officers; and the great canopy of the sky overarching all, came to add its sublimity ever present, but only realized when other great things are occurring beneath each.

But the moral of the scene was its grand point. A sovereign state had been assailed, and she had uttered but a hint, and her sons had hastened to show that they were ready to defend her. Law had been violated by actual murder and attempted treason, and that gibbet was erected by law, and to uphold law was this military force assembled. But, greater still—God's Holy Law and righteous Providence was vindicated, "Thou shalt not kill"—"Whoso sheddeth man's blood, by man shall his blood be shed." And here the gray-haired man of violence meets his fate, after he has seen his two sons cut down before him, in the same career of violence into which he had introduced them. So perish all such enemies of Virginia! All such enemies of the Union! All such foes of the human race! So I felt, and so I said, with solemnity and without one shade of animosity, as I turned to break the silence, to those around me. Yet, the mystery was awful, to see the human form thus treated by men, to see life suddenly stopped in its current, and to ask one's self the question without answer—"And what then?"

In all that array there was not, I suppose, one throb of sympathy for the offender. All felt in the depths of their hearts that it was right. On the other hand, there was not one single word or gesture of exultation or of insult. From the beginning to the end, all was marked by the most absolute decorum and solemnity. There was no military music, no saluting by troops as they passed one another, nor anything done for show. The criminal hung upon the gallows for nearly forty minutes, and after being examined by a whole staff of surgeons, was deposited in a neat coffin to be delivered to his friends, and transported to Harpers Ferry, where his wife awaited it. She came in company with two persons to see her husband last night, and returned to Harpers Ferry this morning. She is described by those who saw her as a very large, masculine woman, of absolute composure of manner. The officers who witnessed their meeting in the jail said they met as if nothing unusual had taken place, and had a comfortable supper together.

Brown would not have the assistance of any Minister in jail during his last days, nor their presence with him on the scaffold. In going from prison to the place of execution, he said very little, only assuring those who were with him that he had no fear, nor had he at any time in his life, known what fear was. When he entered the gate of the enclosure, he expressed his admiration of the beauty of the surrounding country, and pointing to different residences, asked who were the owners of them.

There was a very small crowd to witness the execution. Governor Wise and General Taliaferro had both issued proclamations exhorting the citizens to remain at home and guard their property, and warned them of possible danger. The train on the Winchester Railroad had been stopped from carrying passengers; and even passengers on the Baltimore Railroad were subjected to examination and detention. An arrangement was made to divide the expected crowed into recognized citizens, and those not recognized; to require the former to go to the right, and the latter to the left. Of the latter there was not a single one. It was told last night there were not in Charles Town ten persons besides citizens and military.

There is but one opinion as to the completeness of the arrangements made on the occasion, and the absolute success with which they were carried out. I have said something about the striking effect of the pageant as a pageant, but the excellence of it was that everything was arranged solely with the view of efficiency, and not for effect upon the eye. Had it been intended as a mere spectacle, it could not have been made more imposing, or had actual need occurred, it was the best possible arrangement.

You may be inclined to ask was all this necessary? I have not time to enter upon the question now. Governor Wise thought it necessary, and he said he had reliable information. The responsibility of calling out the force rests with him. It only remained for those under his orders to dispose the force in the best manner. That this was done is unquestionable, and, whatever credit is due for it, may fairly be claimed by those who accomplished it.

Witnessing such a dramatic and historic event would have left quite an impression on the young cadets. Though Brown's assault was on a federal arsenal, it had occurred on Virginia soil, and it was Virginia's Governor Wise who had signed Brown's death warrant. Brown's offense was as much against Virginia as it was against the Union; thus, Preston's theatrical proclamation of: "So perish all such enemies of Virginia! All such enemies of the Union!"

Headstone of John Thomas Lewis Preston. *Photo by author.*

Brown's actions and subsequent hanging, along with growing abolitionist sentiment in the North and Brown's elevation to martyr status, would certainly have been at the center of many conversations in the months to follow. These cadets came to believe, as Superintendent Smith and others did, that "northern abolitionists, by their inflammatory writings and speeches, were encouraging slaves to commit insurrection and murder." Stonewall Jackson biographer and eminent Civil

previous chapter could have easily been the impetus for a "mini Civil War" in Lexington. And how the incident concluded gives us a glimpse of the leadership and mettle of VMI's favorite son. James Robertson sets the scene of the confrontation:

> *Unionists and secessionists—basically in the form of Captain Samuel Letcher's militia company and VMI cadets, respectively—got the idea at the same time to raise a flag of loyalty near the county courthouse. The cadets acted first, marching into the middle of town where a pro-Union crowd four times their number stood in open hostility. Some individual threats went back and forth, a one-on-one altercation flared here and there, but the situation remained in an uneasy calm.*

The cadets went first, running their flag up the pole and listening to some speeches. The Unionists then raised their flag, unaware that some cadets had weakened their pole by boring several holes through it near the base the night before. As soon as Old Glory stiffened in the breeze, the pole snapped off and came crashing down on spectators, causing minor injuries to a few of those gathered. The cadets cheered and headed back to VMI for the evening meal. As they were finishing their supper, a cadet burst into the mess hall and shouted, "House Mountain men have fallen on some of the cadets uptown and killed them!" The report was completely false, but none took the time to confirm. Within minutes, 180 angry young men armed with muskets were running toward Main Street. Superintendent Smith, weak and recovering from pneumonia, attempted in vain to stop them. As the cadets were ordered into formation by cadet captain Thomas S. Galloway, they loaded their muskets, fixed bayonets and faced a large mob of pro-Union citizens. VMI professors James Woods Massie and Raleigh Edward Colston both made pleas for the cadets to stand down and return to their barracks. Their pleas were ignored.

Then, seemingly out of nowhere, there appeared a figure—shoulders stooped, jaw set, steel-blue eyes ablaze and piercing. He spoke not a word but paced back and forth in front of the young men, looking as many as he could directly in the eye. In Jennings's account, he states that "his stature straightened and grew taller and bigger, and his merit, which was known to all, made him the central figure."

Within minutes, the cadets turned about-face and walked back to the VMI campus. What could not be accomplished with urgent pleas from

Superintendent Smith or Professors Massie and Colston, Major Thomas J. Jackson had accomplished with merely his presence and sternly manifested disapproval. Immediately upon arriving back on campus grounds, Smith called for an assembly. Smith began at once to berate the cadets for "insubordinate conduct." Though Smith had openly supported what he believed to be the constitutional right of secession and had been critical of the North's increasingly "radical abolitionist" posturing, he certainly did not condone this type of behavior; nor did he embrace the cadets' eagerness for war. Seated solemnly behind Smith on the podium were Major Jackson, Major Preston and Professor Massie. Following Smith's stern rebuke, Preston and Massie had their say but were not quite as harsh.

Up to this point, there is no record of Jackson having uttered a word of rebuke to any cadet over the near catastrophe. His dramatic, unexpected appearance at the confrontation on Main Street had been enough to send the cadets, tails tucked between their legs, hustling back to VMI. He had made his statement with his presence, not his words.

According to Jennings Wise's recounting of the assembly meeting, cadets started calling for Jackson to speak to them after Preston and Massie had sat down but notes that "at first Jackson declined to respond and only arose at the reiterated request of Colonel Smith." James Robertson writes that Smith leaned toward Jackson and said, "I have driven the nail, but it needs clinching. Speak with them."

What follows has been dubbed "Stonewall Jackson's Scabbard Speech." Wise recounts what happened next:

> *At once, he mounted the rostrum and faced his audience. His erect figure, flashing eye, energetic expression—short, quick and to the point—disclosed to the commonest mind a leader of merit. He said, "Military men make short speeches, and as for myself, I am no hand at speaking now. The time for war has not yet come, but it will come, and that soon; and when it does come, my advice is to draw the sword and throw away the scabbard."*

Jackson's comments electrified the assembled cadets, and as Jackson turned on his heels and returned to his seat, the assembly exploded with applause and "cheers of approval." With those simple words Jackson had masterfully advised caution while simultaneously offering measured encouragement, and more importantly, he had won the hearts and confidence of the young men assembled before him.

Jennings Wise put it this way:

> *The personality of the speaker, the force of those simple words thus uttered, elicited a response of approval I never heard surpassed, except for the Confederate yell often heard on the battlefield, a little later on. This simple speech and manner of Jackson established in the minds of his audience the belief that he was a leader upon whose loyalty and courage we could rely.*

And James Robertson points out that Jackson's conduct elicited a transformation in how he was perceived by the Corps:

> *No one gave thought to "Tom Fool" Jackson or to the eccentric who had long been the butt of campus jokes. What the cadets saw that night was a ramrod straight, inflexible soldier standing before them…What the cadets heard was an authoritative voice of a quality never before perceived in the major.*

Long through the night, after the cadets had been dismissed, cheers of "Hurrah for Old Jack! He is the right stripe!" could be heard throughout the barracks. Wise concludes his description of the event with these words: "Thus it was, that Major Jackson, 'Old Tom Fool,' sprang into prominence among the cadets as the 'man of the hour' in their military world." It was indeed a transformative and definitive moment and one that would benefit Jackson and the Confederacy in the months ahead.

Then, after a flurry of communications between Richmond and VMI and shortly before dawn on April 21, 1861, the order that many had longed for, and others had dreaded, was received at the institute. Virginia governor Letcher ordered VMI's Corps of Cadets to report immediately to Richmond to serve as drill masters for the new recruits pouring into the state capital. As Francis Smith was in Richmond advising Letcher, Major Preston was acting superintendent of VMI and immediately issued Order Number 63 in response:

> *When the muster is held for men who have souls to defend their native soil from violation, insult and subjugation, the heart of every Virginian responds to the voice, and, with stern delight, he answers, "Here!"*
>
> *Words are not necessary now to stimulate.*
>
> *The Corps of Cadets will prove their birth and breeding, and exhibit to Virginia the work of her favorite Institute. The cadet will not fail to manifest the advantage which the military training gives to him over those*

not less brave than himself. The Corps will go forth the pride of its friends, the hope of the State, and the terror of her foes. May the blessing of the God of Hosts rest upon every one who is battling in this holy cause!

The march will be performed as directed by special order.

In the march, the Corps will be under the command of Major Jackson. Major Colston is assigned to duty as Acting Commandant of Cadets, and will report to Major Jackson. Lieutenant Cunningham will act as Assistant Commandant of Cadets, and will report to Major Colston. Lieutenant McDonald is assigned to the Artillery, and will report to Major Jackson. Lieutenant Semmes will accompany the Corps as Adjutant.

Dr. R.L. Madison, Surgeon, and Dr. J.R. Page, Assistant Surgeon, will comprise the Medical Staff. Assistant Surgeon Page will be with the Corps on the march.

Commissary Gibbs will accompany the Corps as far as Staunton.

By order of the Adjutant-General, Lieutenants McCausland and Shipp will remain here to raise companies.

The details will be prepared, as heretofore ordered, and be ready to be inspected at 10 o'clock.

At 12:30 o'clock they will be formed to march. Dinner at 12 o'clock.

The following detail is made of cadets to form a guard of the Virginia Military Institute.

By order of Major Preston,
T.M. SEMMES,
"Adjutant."

Approximately 176 cadets began readying for the march to Richmond, and the order included a list of 48 younger cadets who were to remain on campus.

After Jackson had made last-minute preparations, he asked his pastor, Dr. William S. White, to offer a benediction for the youthful warriors. It was ten minutes past noon when White concluded his prayer and said, "Amen." As the young men grew anxious, a number began to shout, "Let us go!" Jackson was unmoved. He had his orders. The march was to begin at 12:30 p.m. When the clock rang out at the half hour signaling it was time, Jackson mounted his horse, lined up in front of Company A and shouted, "Attention battalion! Right face! By the file left, march!"

And with that, the cadets of VMI joined their comrades from Washington College. Both Lexington schools would provide some of the most prominent military figures in the Confederate army. But as a result of Lexington being the home of the state's premier military school, it would pay a heavy price.

Chapter 4

Like So Many Savages

The War Comes to Lexington

I seemed to have spent a lifetime in one day.
—Fannie Wilson

Lexington, Va.
June 17, 1864
My dear Papa
You are no doubt anxious to hear what has become of us all since the unexpected arrival of the Yankees and how we were treated by them. On last Thursday we were enjoying undisturbed quiet, having heard the Yankees had suffered a severe defeat from General Breckinridge.

Imagine our surprise and fright on Friday evening when a courier came in stating that McCausland with his small force was at Cedar Grove and the Yankees at Brownsburg. A few minutes later another one brought news that the Yankees had reached Cedar Grove and McCausland had encamped on Colonel Cameron's farm, about three miles from town where they intended remaining for the night. Great excitement prevailed in town; many persons sent off their servants together with wagons loaded with provisions, and nearly all the gentlemen of town went out into the mountains, in that way hoping to escape capture by the enemy; among them the cadets, and professors of both Institute and College with many of the citizens. On Saturday morning McCausland crossed the river and burnt the bridge, he deployed his men on the cliffs of the river above and below the mill where a stubborn resistance was made by our men, who at last retreated.

Meanwhile the Yankees had reached an elevated field just opposite the town and planting their artillery in full range of the main street, they commenced shelling it; afterward assigning as a reason that they wanted to clear the streets of the "Rebels" who were passing up at the time; in which they were much mistaken, for McCausland being aware of their intention retreated up the back street.

The first shell that struck our part of town passed through Mrs. Johnston's house; the next one above ours tearing a circular hole just the size of the ball. We were standing in the front door when the ball passed over our heads, and fearing danger we went to the cellar, thinking that was the safest place, and were standing on the steps when we heard the whizzing near us; we found that another one had passed through our garret wall and struck the rafter, exploding with a thundering noise. It knocked nearly all the plastering off and all the sash out of the windows, made a great many large holes in the wall and floor. One piece passed through the ceiling of the passage, two small pieces perforated the ceiling of grandpa's room just above the head of his bed in which he was lying at the time in a doze, and was aroused by the fall of the plaster. I seemed to have spent a lifetime in one day. I never before had an idea of the terror caused by the shelling of a town, never seemed to realize what it meant.

In a few moments the alarm of fire was given; shells were flying thick and fast. Uncle was the first to run up to the garret and burst the door open where he was almost suffocated by the smoke which was discovered to proceed from the explosion and [not] *from fire as was supposed. Not long after several white flags were hoisted by some of the citizens when the enemy in turn raised one and the firing ceased.*

The Yankees foiled in the expectations of crossing the bridge soon made a good ford and in about half an hour after the shelling ceased, the wretches galloped into the town yelling and whooping like so many savages. We kept the doors locked and the windows closed all the time they were here.

Sunday morning about 10 o'clock the Yankees set fire to the Institute, blew the walls down and destroyed the mess hall and professors' houses, and if General Smith's daughter, Mrs. Morrison, had not been very ill they fully intended destroying his elegant mansion. All the Point property except the miller's and toll houses was burned. Governor Letcher's house was burnt with but five minutes' notice. The Yankees took Mr. Matthew White, Jr. prisoner and he was seen Sunday afternoon marching out of town with a squad of soldiers, who shot him for bush-whacking; all the time deceiving his parents by telling them he was at home. His body was found unburied in the woods near Mrs. Cameron's house on the evening the Yankees left.

Last Wednesday there was scarcely a Yankee to be seen anywhere in town, and our scouts captured the few stragglers that remained. On Tuesday morning I was aroused early by the rumbling of the artillery racing out of town with all its speed; before breakfast the whole front street far as the eye could see up and down was jammed with their wagon trains which seemed to be in the greatest possible hurry, and before 12 o'clock all were gone except a few horsemen who seemed to be left as scouts. We were in high spirits you may know, and there never was so much rejoicing in town.

I have heard of a great deal of destruction by the Yankees and a great many shells have struck houses in town. We heard that Uncle Thomas Wilson was in the woods with his servants and stock when some Yankees fell upon them, wounding him in the head and capturing his wagons, etc. Two of his servants came here night before last bringing us news about him. We hope he will recover. Colonel Massie came home yesterday; said he had seen you and spent a very sick night at your house where he received kind attention for which he seemed very grateful, thinks a great deal of you.

We have it reported here this morning [twentieth] *that the Yankees have gotten a good whipping at Lynchburg and are retreating. I hope they will not come this way. Uncle and Aunt write me in love to yourself, Mama, my brother and sisters and all friends. Do let us hear from you soon. Your affectionate daughter, Fannie M. Lyle Wilson.*

P.S. We heard from Uncle Thomas last night. He was wounded right badly. He eye was shot out and the pistol was placed so near to his face that his hair was burnt. There are several deep saber cuts on his head; his wound is painful but not dangerous. Fannie.

Though official military reports regarding battles are important for historians and subsequent generations to understand such important events, the view presented through the innocence and experience of a sixteen-year-old girl can provide us with another dimension and perspective. Such is the case with the letter written by Miss Fannie M. Lyle Wilson to her father describing the fear she experienced and the destruction she witnessed during Union general David "Black Dave" Hunter's raid on Lexington in June 1864. This young girl's letter serves as a good introduction to Lexington's most memorable experience of the American Civil War. Sadly, Fannie would die a year after writing her letter.

Confederate general John McCausland. *Library of Congress.*

Other than McCausland's small command, the home guard and the remaining VMI cadets, the town was, for all practical purpose, defenseless when Hunter's army—eighteen thousand strong—began their march toward Lexington from nearby Staunton on June 10. Lexington was only about forty miles south of Staunton, and already reports were circulating in the community that the Yankees were on their way. Though Confederate skirmishers slowed their advance south through the tiny villages of Middlebrook, Newport and Brownsburg, Union forces progressed slowly toward Lexington. On their way, they burned several flour mills—two at Greenville, one at Midway and one at Fairfield. As news traveled up the Valley Pike and along the network of neighboring valley farms, citizens scurried to hide stores and valuables in their attics and barns and under floorboards—even in their outhouses. Historian Robert Driver recounted how even children got involved in the effort to save possessions:

> *Calvin Culton and a black companion were playing at the family home on Hays Creek when he heard the cry, "The Yankees are coming!" The youths raced to the house, where they were joined by a second Culton son. The three were handed hams from the smoke house with orders to conceal them from the despicable marauders. The youths rode into the woods with the prized meat, which they placed in a sink hole and covered with rocks.*
>
> *The three hid in the woods with the horses overnight. When they emerged the next morning, they beheld a shocking sight. The figure of an old man was dangling from a tree.*

Cured hams were a prized target of both Confederate and Union foragers due to their ease of transport, value for nourishment and the fact that they would keep for long periods of time. Most Shenandoah Valley farms kept a good supply on hand and became quite inventive in ways to conceal these items from both armies. A member of the Cochran family related a story to me that involves the longtime and prominent family of Staunton and Augusta County. As Hunter's army was leaving Staunton, they stopped at Folly Farm, which was at the time, and still is, owned by the Cochran family. The farm is quite prominent from the road and would have been an easy target from the Valley Pike. The farm was founded by Joseph Smith in 1818 and is still located about two miles south of Staunton on Route 11 (the Valley Pike and today Lee-Jackson Highway). The farm's most striking feature is a serpentine wall that was designed by Thomas Jefferson. According to family lore, as it became apparent that Hunter's army would eventually pass Folly Farm, servants and family members gathered up all the hams in storage. The Yankees soon arrived and demanded food stores. The family handed over some items in hopes of pacifying the soldiers. But they wanted more—specifically meat, but there was none to be found. Giving up, they formed back in column and marched off the premises, not realizing there were several hams tied to ropes and hanging in a spruce tree over their heads.

Another Yankee-foiling, and somewhat humorous, incident occurred on the Cochran farm. After getting separated from his scouting unit, Confederate captain John Newton Opie decided to hide out in the woods at Folly Farm. His location gave him a good view of the Valley Pike, and he could hear and see any Federals approaching from a good distance off. Union troops were everywhere, and he needed to lie low until most of the Federal army had moved south. Opie recounts what happened:

> *Five miles south of Staunton, on the Lexington road, is an old-fashioned brick mansion, the residence of Col. James C. Cochran. The grounds are enclosed by a brick wall, and the dwelling is about one hundred and fifty yards from the main road, which is reached by a wide avenue. South of the house is a large barn, in rear of which, and running parallel with the main road, is a dense forest. I took a position in this woods, where I had a full view of the road...For two or three hours, I watched the army pass by, consisting of cavalry, infantry and artillery, hoping to see a break in the column that I might dash through. I was so close to them, that I could hear their conversation. At last, I saw*

Confederate captain John Opie. *Author's collection.*

an officer leave the column and ride up the avenue. I was very lonesome, and determined to enjoy this man's company, nolens volens; so, mounting my horse, I drew my six-shooter, and rode slowly and cautiously out to the edge of the woods. There was the Federal officer, a magnificent looking fellow, standing in full view, his horse a few steps from him, quietly grazing. Forth from the forest, like a projectile from a gun, I rushed up to the brick wall, and leveling my pistol at him, I commanded him to surrender. He placed his hand on his pistol and shook it loose in the holster. "Draw, and you are a dead man!" I exclaimed. "Surrender, or I will fire," accompanied by an expletive. The man looked longingly at his people, then at my face. He saw I had the drop on him, and he remarked, "I surrender." "Unbuckle your belt and hand it to me," I commanded, not taking my eyes from him; and, with pistol still presented, I reached out for his belt with my left hand, when, hastily, taking his holster from his belt, which I dropped, I transferred it to mine. While I was thus engaged, my ears were greeted with the rush of cavalry thundering down the avenue. "Mount your horse and ride as hard as you can drive," I said; "and, unless I speak, keep straight for the woods," and away we went out of the yard, as the Federal cavalry dashed up to the front. But they were too late. After riding, at full speed, for about a mile, we halted, dismounted, and tied our horses upon a high hill, from which I had a full view of the surrounding country. "Let us lie here and rest," I observed; "and won't you tell me your name?" "I am Captain Johnson, of Crook's staff, and also correspondent of the Wheeling Intelligencer,*" he said. I told him my name, and, for several hours, enjoyed the conversation of my agreeable prisoner.*

Others in the path of the Federals' march to Lexington were not as fortunate as the occupants of Folly Farm. Calvin Colton later claimed that the Yankees stole thirteen horses from his grandfather, as well as the smokehouse meat and all of the family's milk and butter. Another local resident, David Blackwood, had all his horses stolen as well. The

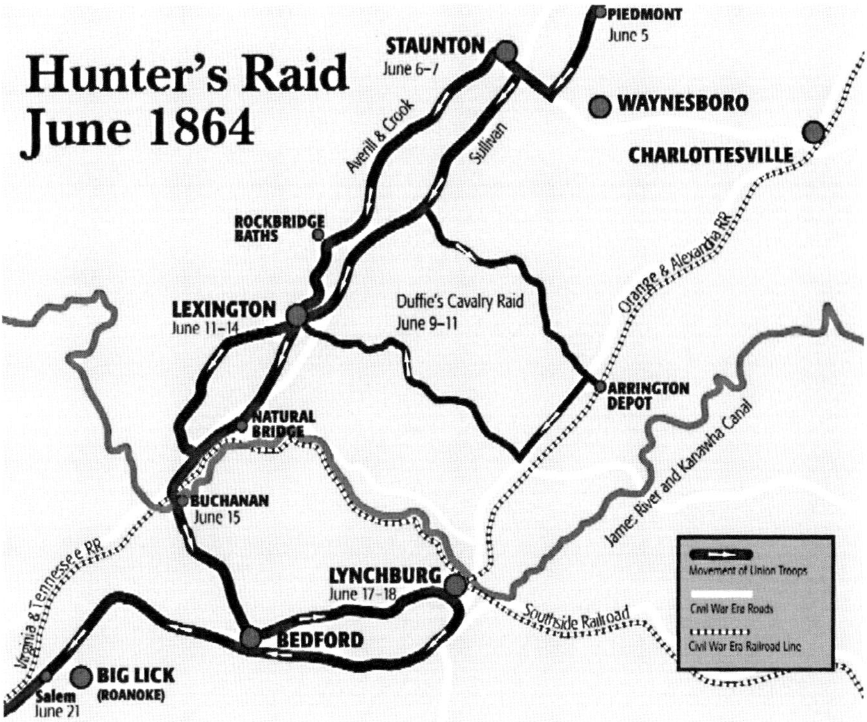

Map of Hunter's Raid. *Hunter's Raid Tourism Partnership.*

marauding Federals butchered cattle, sheep and hogs as needed without compensation or concern for the citizens of Augusta and Rockbridge Counties. Author Gary Walker, in his book *Hunter's Fiery Raid Through the Virginia Valleys*, points out that "Union soldiers at the rear hardly took notice of the fighting. They took 'all the cattle and horses that can be found.'"

But many of the residents in Lexington had enough warning that they were able to secret some of their livestock away and hide it in the Blue Ridge Mountains. They further prepared for the coming invasion by bolting their doors, nailing their windows shut and fastening the shutters. Women and children sought protection in the basements of their homes. As Hunter's army was approaching Lexington, some of the VMI cadets who had remained in Lexington stacked turpentine-soaked hay bales on the bridge that crossed the North River into town. As McCausland's men crossed the bridge, they set the hay bales on fire. At about the same time, a Federal battery took up position on some high ground overlooking the bridge and across the river from the institute as thick, black smoke and flames shot skyward from the burning bridge. On the parade ground at VMI, a cadet battalion began dueling with the Federals across the river as burning timbers from the bridge splashed into the North River. One cadet would write that "we were nearly in the line of fire of the shots directed at out battery. A number of shells struck the parade ground, some exploding there, and others ricocheting over our heads."

Viewed by the opposing armies as more of an artillery duel and sharpshooter's contest than a real battle, the citizens of Lexington remembered it quite differently. The Union forces had, only a few days before, been engaged in fierce fighting at Piedmont. This contest simply did not compare. But for many citizens not accustomed to war, it was a terrifying experience. As there was never any question about the outcome of Hunter's raid, Superintendent Smith, along with the remaining VMI cadets, as well as McCausland's army, began retreating about 1:00 p.m. The shelling continued until mid-afternoon. As women and children huddled in basements, homes near VMI were struck. Local resident Cornelia McDonald wrote, "Some shells went through the houses, frightening the inhabitants terribly…Our house was struck in several places." And Maggie Preston wrote:

> *We have been shelled in reply all day; one shell exploded in our orchard, a few yards beyond us—our house being just in their range as they threw them at the retreating Confederates…The people from the lower part of town fled from their dwellings, and our house was filled with women and children. Just in the midst of the thickest shelling, the poor wounded boy from the Institute hospital was carried here, surrounded by a guard of Cadets. He had borne the removal well. I have distributed some of J.'s* [J.T.L. Preston] *blackberry wine, which I have always forborne to open, among the frightened and almost fainting ladies.*

Mrs. William Nelson Pendleton gave the following account to her husband:

> *The wretches shelled the town for hours. Shells fell everywhere in the town—Colonel Williamsons' yard, into Mr. John Campbell's house, into Miss Baxter's house. One struck Colonel Reid's front door and almost struck his daughter…one fell in the garden here; one struck somewhere near us, as several small bullets were found in the upper porch here and at Captain Moore's.*

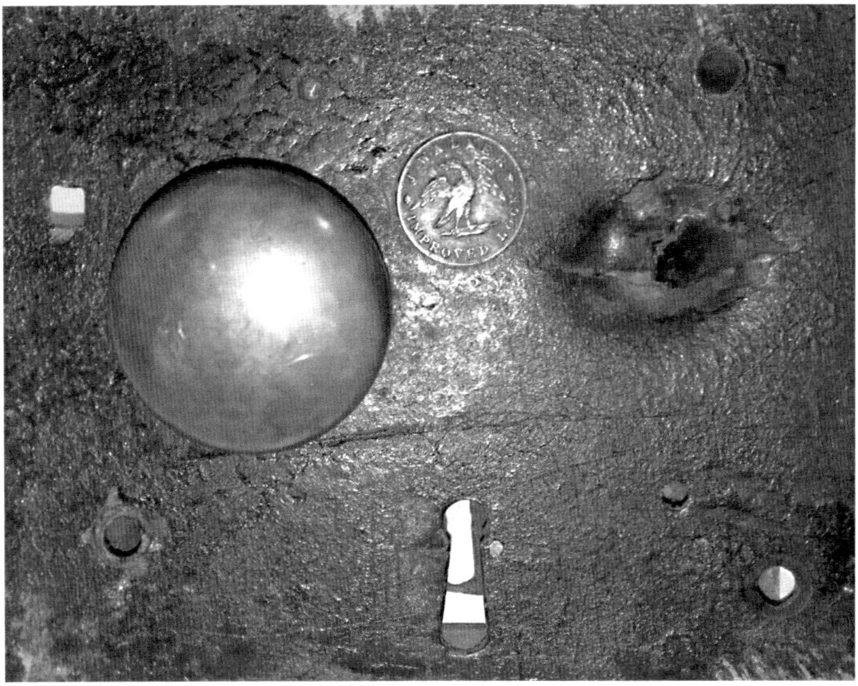

Doorknob and plate of Professor J.L. Campbell damaged during the shelling of Lexington. *Special Collections, Leyburn Library, Washington and Lee University, photo by author.*

William S. White, Stonewall Jackson's pastor, also wrote of what he had witnessed:

> *Twenty houses were struck, some of which were seriously damaged, and two were ignited, but the fire was extinguished. Six shells passed over the parsonage, one exploded in the garden, and one in the stable-yard. But not a person was struck. Many very narrowly escaped.*

White later described Hunter as "a man whose notoriety among our people made him terrible to the timid and detestable to all." White later wrote that he had also suffered personal loss: "They robbed me of my corn and hay worth $500. They cut the curtains from my carriage and carried off a portion of the harness." A slave belonging to White named John told White, "Master, these yankees are the beat of all the rogues I ever saw, black or white."

With no armed resistance left in Lexington, the destruction and looting soon began in earnest. Cadet John Sergeant Wise later wrote:

> *With heavy hearts we passed through the town, bidding adieu to such of its residents as we had known in happier days. Our route was southward to Balcony Falls, which we reached late that evening. At a high point, probably five miles south of Lexington, we came in full sight of our old home. The day was bright and clear, and we saw the towers and turrets of the barracks, mess-hall, and professors' houses in full blaze, sending up great masses of flame and smoke. The only building on the entire reservation not destroyed by fire was the residence of General Smith. His daughter was very ill, and as the physicians declared it would cost her life to remove her, the house was spared through the intercession of Colonel Du Pont. No words could describe our feelings as we rested on the roadside, and watched the conflagration. The place was endeared by a thousand memories.*

After the Confederate forces left town, the shelling ceased, gunfire became sporadic and distant and "a strange quiet" settled over Lexington. But that was short-lived. Cornelia McDonald wrote that the retreating Confederates had left "the terror-stricken people to their fears, and to the tender mercies of the enemy." Those mercies would be in short supply.

Some of the Federals began making their way slowly and carefully over the charred remains of the bridge, others had forded farther up river. Soon a pontoon bridge was constructed where the original bridge had stood, allowing for the remainder of the army to cross into Lexington. The Yankees soon overran the town. Maggie Preston chronicled what she witnessed, revealing her indignation and mettle:

> *Then the infantry began to pour in: there remained behind, and with cavalry who came in after, flooded the town. They began to pour into our yard and kitchen. I ordered them out of the kitchen, half a dozen at a time, and hesitated not to speak in the most firm and commanding tone to them. At first they were content to receive bacon, two slices apiece; but they soon became insolent; demanded the smokehouse key, and told me they would break the door unless I opened it. I protested against their pillage, and with a score of them surrounding me, with guns in their hands, proceeded to the smokehouse and threw it open, entreating that at the same time, by the respect they had for their wives,*

> *mothers, and sisters, to leave me a little meat. They heeded me no more than wild beasts would have done; swore at me; and left me not one piece. Some rushed down the cellar steps, seized the newly churned butter there, and made off. I succeeded in keeping them out of the house. We have no dinner; managed to procure a little supper; we have nailed up all the windows. I wrote a polite note to Gen. Averell, asking for a guard; none was sent.*

William Nelson Pendleton's daughter, Rose, described what she saw:

> *For two hours there was one continuous stream of cavalry, riding at a fast trot, and several abreast, passing out at the top of town. A quarter after four the vile rabble came over the hills in swarms and the feeling* [of] *the poor Lexington people may be better imagined than described. They advanced into the town on three roads, and came shouting as though they had captured some valuable post. I must not forget to state after our men passed three houses hoisted white flags of surrender.*

Like Mrs. Preston, other ladies of Lexington proved their grit in protecting their firesides. Mrs. Pendleton's disgust with the pillagers, and her determination to stand up to the Yankee invaders when they showed up at the Episcopal parsonage, is quite evident in this description penned by daughter Rose:

> *We were soon overrun by the thieving wretches. We kept the house doors all locked except the front door and while some 2 or 3 of us kept guard there Mama stationed herself with her keys at the back door leading into the kitchen. The first who came asked for something to eat. Ma gave them all the bread and buttermilk she had, and a shoulder of bacon, which had been cooked for Sunday dinner. They were insolent as possible, cursed and swore, vowed they would have anything and everything they wanted, but still Ma was so firm and we showed so plainly that we were not afraid of them, that they were forced to go off not intimidating us.*

Of course, not all women were as confrontational as Maggie Preston and the Pendleton ladies. Cornelia McDonald's home took a different approach:

> *We remained as quiet as possible all the afternoon while the town was alive with soldiers plundering and robbing the inhabitants. Some came into our*

> *yard, robbed the milkhouse of its contents and passed on their way, picking up everything they could use or destroy.*

Reverend William S. White hinted that such malevolent looting and destruction of property was due to the spiritual condition of some of the Yankees. In his book *Lexington Presbyterian Church, 1789–1989*, Robert F. Hunter writes:

> *White moved freely among the Federal troops, talking with as many as he could. "It was very obvious that there were several distinct parties in their army," he observed, "differing widely in their principles." He was chagrined to find that no chaplain accompanied them. When he asked a major about it, his reply was, "O yes, we have a great many; almost one to every regiment." White answered, "I am astonished that you have no worship to-day." The major replied, "Our chaplains are not of much account. They seldom or never preach. I have not heard a sermon, or even a prayer, for many months."*

White observed that the war had made the spiritual health of most people either better or worse. Evidently, it was a case of the latter for many of the Union soldiers occupying Lexington. White's opinion was further influenced by General Hunter's conduct, particularly what White viewed as a callous disregard for women and children:

> *He seemed to riot in the alarm excited by his presence among women and children. In two cases, when respectfully applied to in person by ladies of the highest refinement and greatest prudence, for some protection against his ruffian troops, who were tramping through their houses, destroying or bearing off their food and furniture, not leaving the apparel and bedding of their infant children, he replied to one of these ladies with a brutality that would have disgraced a savage: "These are the natural consequences of war, and you must bear them as best you can." To the other he said: "I know your father and brothers; look to them to protect you."*
>
> *"Thus encouraged, the work of ruin went on, especially in the houses of these two ladies, until scarcely a morsel, and, in one, not a morsel of food was left, and scarcely an article of apparel or bed-covering was left."*

The women of Lexington seemed to be more insulted at having strangers who spoke with a nasal twang rifle through their drawers and bed linens than they did at having their homes shelled. The "collateral" shelling might well be forgiven as "the natural consequences of war," but having a Yankee soldier fondle a Southern woman's underwear was quite another story. To the pious Scots-Irish of Lexington, Virginia, such callous disregard for even a hint of honor—particularly when it concerned women and children—was something they were not accustomed to seeing, especially among those in authority. This conduct would color their perception of Northerners for generations.

Even the Lord's Day offered no reprieve from the assault on private property. Maggie Preston made the following entry in her diary on Sunday, June 12, 1861:

> *I slept undisturbed during the night, but was called down stairs early this morning by the servants, who told me the throng of soldiers could not be kept out of the house. I went down and appealed to them as a lone woman who had nobody to protect her.* [I] *might as well have appealed to bricks. I left the smokehouse door open, to let them see that every piece of meat was taken (I had some hid under the porch, which as yet had not been found). They came into the dining room, and began to carry away the china, when a young fellow from Philadelphia (he said) took the dishes from them, and made them come out. I told them I was a Northern lineage woman, but confessed I was ashamed of my Northern lineage when I saw them come on such an errand. They demanded to be let in the cellar, and one fellow threatened me with the burning of the house if I did not just what they demanded. I said, "Yes, we are at your mercy—burn it down—but I won't give you the key." My children were crying for something to eat; I had nothing to feed them but crackers.*

Robert Driver notes that Mrs. Preston was then delivered the news that "all of the sheep had been slaughtered and the cattle and horses taken by the Federals." As bad as the treatment of Lexington's civilians by Hunter's army, it paled in comparison to what Virginia Military Institute experienced. Superintendent Francis Smith opened his report of July 15, 1864, with the following words:

> *On the Sabbath morning of June 12, the beautiful buildings erected by the liberality of the state for her favored military school, were made a mass of*

ruins by the order of Major General D. Hunter, commanding U.S. Army of Western Virginia, after having been first sacked by his lawless and rapacious soldiery.

Some destruction to buildings at VMI had already occurred during the first hours of shelling. But that was just the beginning. Mrs. Preston wrote in her diary that the Federals "set fire to the Institute about 9 o'clock [Sunday, June 12]. The flames are now enveloping it; the towers have fallen; the arsenal is exploding as I write." David Hunter Strother, who was both General Hunter's cousin and his chief of staff, made the following observation about the burning of VMI:

> *The burning of the Institute made a grand picture, a vast volume of black smoke rolled above the flames and covered half the horizon…The institute burnt out about 2 p.m. and the arsenal blew up with a smart explosion. The General* [Hunter] *seemed to enjoy the scene and turning to me expressed his great satisfaction at having me with him.*

Not all of the Federals viewed the destruction of the "West Point of the South" as a "grand picture." In an article titled "David Hunter: The General Who Burned VMI," which appeared in the *VMI Alumni Review* (Spring 1997), historian Edward A. Miller notes:

> *Some officers, such as Col. Rutherford B. Hayes, a future president; Capt. Henry A. Du Pont, a future senator; and Lt. Col. Charles G. Halpine, Hunter's adjutant, opposed the destruction. The latter wrote in his diary that he was heartsick to see the Institute destroyed but that he could not change Hunter's decision. Halpine was on the hill to view the spectacle, and he wrote, "How I wish it were over."*

Robert Driver points out one account that could lead one to conclude that Hunter's enthusiasm for VMI's destruction bordered on the sadistic:

> *A member of the First New York (Lincoln) Cavalry recorded Hunter's demeanor as he studied the execution of his order. "He stood looking at the burning building, saying as he rubbed his hands and chuckled with delight, "Doesn't it burn beautifully?"*

Chief of Staff Strother, when asked by Hunter for his opinion on burning VMI later recounted:

> *I told him I looked upon it as a most dangerous establishment where treason was systematically taught. That I believed the States Rights conspirators had with subtlety and forethought established and encouraged the school for the express purpose of educating the youth of the county into such opinions as would render them ready and efficient tools wherewith to overthrow the government of the country when the hour and opportunity arrived…The catalogue of the Institute itself showed what a list of capable military officers had been there raised up against the government of the country. This was the great paramount reason for its destruction by fire.*

Hunter burned a total of five structures in Lexington, four directly related to VMI: the cadet hospital, the barracks and two sets of faculty quarters. And upon receiving a copy of a proclamation issued by former governor Letcher that, according to Strother, incited "the people to arise and wage a guerrilla warfare upon the vandal hordes of Yankee invaders," Hunter issued an immediate order to burn Letcher's home. Cornelia McDonald entered the following description of the burning of the Letcher home in her diary:

> *Mrs. Letcher had consented to entertain two officers at her house, that she had been civilly asked to do. They had spent the night, and eaten breakfast with the family, socially chatting all the while.*
>
> *When they rose from breakfast, one of them, Capt. Berry, informed Mrs. Letcher that he should immediately set fire to her house. He took a bottle of benzene, or some flammable fluid, and pouring it on the sofas and curtains in the lower rooms, applied a match and then proceeded up stairs. Mrs. Letcher as soon as she became aware of his purpose, ran up stairs, and snatching her sleeping baby from the cradle, rushed from the house with it, leaving everything she had to the flames. Lizzie* [oldest daughter] *ran up stairs and went into her father's room to secure some of his clothes, and had hung over her arm some of his linen, when Capt. Berry came near her with a lighted match, and set fire to the clothes as they hung on her arm. He then gathered all the family clothing and bedding into a pile in the middle of the room and set fire to them.*
>
> *When I reached the scene, Mrs. Letcher was sitting on a stone in the street with her baby on her lap sleeping, and her other little children gathered*

Francis H. Smith's headstone. *Photo by author.*

The Board of Visitors assembles under peculiar circumstance today. On the Sabbath morning of June 12, the beautiful buildings erected by the liberality of the state for her favored military school, were made a mass of ruins by the order of Major General D. Hunter, commanding U.S. Army of Western Virginia, after having been first sacked by his lawless and rapacious soldiery.

The quarters and offices of the Superintendent alone remain; and the order for the destruction of these was only suspended.

Smith then provides some detail about the destruction visited on VMI:

Every species of public property was removed or wantonly destroyed; and among the most serious losses are to be named our valuable library—the accumulated care of twenty-five years—and the philosophical apparatus, so long used by our late distinguished professor of Natural and Experimental Philosophy, Lieut. General Thomas J. Jackson.

Our hospital was first rifled of all of its most valuable medical stores, and was then burnt, although one severely wounded cadet and one sick cadet, dependent upon both for comfort and almost for life, had to be removed from the building at great risk, in the midst of the shelling and the rifle balls of the sharpshooters.

The families of Colonels Williamson and Gilham were required by rude officials to vacate their quarters; and although they were allowed the privilege of removing their furniture, in part, through the kind interposition of the Hon. S. McD. Moore, few facilities were afforded them to do so; and the torch was applied while helpless females were endeavoring to save their little stores, and their quarters and many of their personal effects were destroyed…

…My private library was rifled of many of its most valuable and portable volumes, and the portraits of Ex-Governors McDowell, Wise and Letcher, which occupied prominent positions in it, were removed.

The houses of our poorest operatives, including seamstresses, laundresses and laborers, were searched, in common with those of the citizens generally, and some of these persons were left in a destitute and almost starving condition. The kindness of friends in Lexington had opened their houses to receive the trunks and effects of cadets. Such houses were made the peculiar objects of vindictive spoliation.

Our shoe shop was despoiled of all of its leather and unfinished work, and the shoe lasts, implements and benches were there wantonly destroyed. The bell attached to our public clock was taken down and removed…

> *I have been particular in the recital I have given of the conduct of the enemy to his institution, because I desire to give permanence to the record of infamy which has immortalized the U.S. Army of Western Virginia here.*

Smith then lays out a case as to why he believes most of the VMI buildings should have been spared and how, in his mind, Hunter's army had violated the rules of war:

> *No one, therefore, belonging to the institution can complain that the rules of war should be applied to an establishment marked by such evidences of identification with our revolutionary struggle. It was to have been expected that the cadets should be pursued, that they might be either killed or captured. They asked no immunities from the rigors of war meted to others. The arms and munitions of war were proper subjects for capture or destruction. Its public buildings might have been held by the enemy as a barracks or hospital, and the school itself dispersed. But modern history is appealed to in vain for a like instance of devastation, as marked the track of the invader here…*
>
> *General Hunter commanded an organized army of the United States, whose professed mission was the "restoration of the Union"; and yet it was by his order, and against the remonstrances (as I understand) of some of his own general officers, that the public buildings of the Virginia Military Institute were committed to the flames…Not satisfied with desolation, its walls were polluted with the most obscene language in association with the names of men from Ohio, Pennsylvania, New York, and Massachusetts.*

Though human life was, for the most part, spared during the Lexington raid, two casualties must be noted. The first one is described in the letter by young Fannie Wilson. Matthew White Jr. had, at the beginning of the war, been a captain in the First Rockbridge Dragoons, but poor health required him to leave the Confederate army near the end of 1862. He rejoined the army on June 10, 1864, and, along with some other picketers, shot and killed a fellow Virginian who was acting as a guide for Hunter's army as it made its way through Rockbridge County. After Lexington was captured, White returned home for personal reasons; he was promptly identified, arrested and taken to a nearby farm where he was shot in the back eight times.

By Monday, June 13, the looting and vandalism began to subside, but not before the town newspaper, the *Gazette*, had its printing equipment damaged.

VMI barracks after Hunter's raid. *VMI Archives.*

VMI cadets with Major William Gilham's burned residence in the background, circa 1866. *VMI Archives.*

Finally, on the morning of June 14, the last regiments of the Union army left Lexington—with VMI's bronze statue of Washington, two cadet battalion guns and six French cannons in tow. Despite having its press equipment damaged the *Gazette*, by the fifteenth, was able to print a summation of what Lexington and the Shenandoah Valley had suffered at the hands of Hunter's army:

Stonewall Jackson's grave, circa 1866. *Special Collections, Leyburn Library, Washington and Lee University.*

> *During their march through the Valley, they subsisted upon the people. Families were stripped of all their flour, meat, corn, lard, butter and indeed everything laid up for the support. They made no discrimination between the families of Unionists and Secessionists. They plundered all, and declared their purpose to reduce the people to subjugation, by starvation, if their purposes could be accomplished… The enemy themselves declared that the people here—men, women and children, had shown no sympathy for the Union, or for them and that the rebel feeling was stronger here than in any other County they had passed thro'.*

As the last remnants of Hunter's army left town, and as smoke rose from the ashes, many of Lexington's citizens began to pick up the pieces of what remained of their lives. The smell of charred buildings was thick in the summer air. Many were in shock. Only the year before, they had witnessed the funeral of one of their favorite sons and what many believed was not only the burial of Stonewall Jackson but also of any hopes the Confederacy had in securing independence. Now, VMI lay in ruins, Washington College had been ransacked and vandalized, food stores had been depleted, family heirlooms stolen, homes shelled and burned, livestock stolen or slaughtered, fortunes ruined and honor humiliated. A dark pall hung over the once picturesque "Athens of the South."

Yet a spark of spirit remained in the townspeople of Lexington. They would rebuild, and they would remember.

Chapter 5

African Americans Make Their Mark

And ye shall know the truth, and the truth shall make you free.
—John 8:32

There has been, sadly, more history lost than preserved when it comes to the history of Lexington's African Americans during the time of the Civil War. Even so, there were quite a few blacks—both slave and free—who made their mark. Due to slavery, and the societal realities of the nineteenth century, this history can be complicated to sift through, sort and interpret. What motivated the actions of blacks was, for obvious reasons, much different than what motivated the actions of whites—regardless of whether those actions can be interpreted as pro-Confederate or pro-Union. Certainly, many Lexington blacks hoped and prayed for Union victory—even assisting that effort when they thought it safe to do so—believing a Union victory would mean certain freedom and a better life. Others, though in a very small minority, rooted for the Southern cause and, to some degree, for the same reasons as whites: they were protecting their homes. Others showed sympathy to their Confederate masters to prove loyalty, hoping this might lead to better treatment or even freedom after the war. And some even assisted the Confederate cause for self-preservation, disliking the Yankee invaders almost as much as white Southerners did. That sentiment was expressed by a slave at Virginia Military Institute. During Union general Hunter's raid, a black man who served as VMI's baker, known as Anderson, was asked after the raid if "he had made himself known as belonging to the state." He replied promptly, "No, indeed—if I had told the Yankees that, black living in Lexington at the time the Civil War broke out. Megan Haley Newman noted in an unpublished manuscript that there was a free black named James Humbles who was, before and after the war, employed as the town engineer for Lexington, maintaining the town's waterworks. Robert Driver writes in his book on the First Virginia Cavalry that these were the same man. And muster rolls confirm that Humbles was a "free negro" and enlisted in Lexington as a bugler in the Rockbridge Dragoons, Company C, on April 18, 1861. The following remarks were made on Humbles's muster roll: "Free negro. Mustering officer thinks this man should not be mustered in." Apparently, the rank and file disagreed with their superior, and Humbles was mustered into the ranks. Driver quotes an unidentified source in his notes on Humbles: "For some time during the war he carried his musket and saw active service." Perhaps Humbles's employment in Lexington prior to the war confirmed his "worthiness" in the eyes of his fellow Confederate soldiers.

What we might assume at first glance, while remaining cognizant of whatever preconceptions we may hold, is not always the reality. The stories are often, as we are wont to say, "complicated." One such story involves Jefferson Shields, also known as "Uncle" Jefferson or "Jeff" Shields. Shields is most widely known as Stonewall Jackson's cook. His iconic image is also one of the most recognizable and frequently published of blacks who ostensibly supported the Confederacy. Shields was born a slave in 1829. He became a favorite of Confederate Veterans' groups, attending many reunions and special events after the war. While in attendance at a reunion of the survivors of the Stonewall Brigade in Staunton, Virginia, "Uncle Jeff" was voted in as a member of the brigade and authorized to wear one of the brigade's badges. According to local historian Henry Boley, Shields was proud to attend these meetings and display the medals the old Confederates would give him:

> *Uncle Jeff attended all Confederate reunions in many parts of the South, where he was always the recipient of much attention, about which he talked freely…After each reunion he had a fresh supply of medals and when he would proudly open his coat to display them he looked like the Kaiser on parade.*

Was Shields's "pride" sincere, or was it contrived for fame and acceptance? Was it some of both? We can only surmise based on what we know about Shields and postwar race relations. On the surface,

Jefferson Shields, circa 1900. *Special Collections, Leyburn Library, Washington and Lee University.*

Shields's enthusiasm for being associated with the Confederacy appears sincere. It may well have been. But as many historians have pointed out, that consideration must be tempered with the realities of the society in which Shields lived. It must also be tempered with the fact that Shields is reputed to have been compensated financially for his attendance at the various veterans' meetings.

Numerous articles and books claim that Shields served as Stonewall Jackson's "body servant" or "personal servant" and cook during the war. These claims have been made by historian and Jackson biographer Lenoir Chambers, as well as by Professor Ervin L. Jordan in his classic work *Black Confederates and Afro-Yankees in Civil War Virginia*. Shields's claims were apparently accepted at face value by many Lexingtonians and veterans after the war. The Stonewall Jackson Headquarters Museum in Winchester, Virginia, has displayed a photograph of Shields with the caption: "Jeff Shields, Jackson's aid and cook." There are, however, no Civil War–era records or accounts of Jackson, nor any of his staff, mentioning Jefferson Shields. That does not necessarily prove that Shields never cooked a meal for Jackson's staff, but it does cast doubt on Shields's claims that he served Jackson personally or with any regularity. Shields also professed to have cooked not only for Jackson but also for J.E.B. Stuart. Again, while there is nothing to dispute this, no verifiable historical records exist that would prove the claim either.

Shields's service in the Confederacy *is*, however, verifiable. Shields was the personal body servant and slave of Colonel James Kerr Edmonson of Lexington, not Jackson. Edmonson was commander of the Twenty-seventh Virginia, and his family owned Shields from his birth until the end of the war. It is certainly within the realm of possibility that Shields counted his service in the Stonewall Brigade as "cooking for Stonewall." But that is conjecture.

Another of Shields's claims was that he was the first member of Jackson's famous black Sunday school class:

> *I was General Jackson's first scholar. Somebody ought to write a history of Jackson's Christian life, for he was the greatest Christian that ever lived. Jackson had a class of boys, about eighteen. Jackson kept me from swearing, and I had to go to the Presbyterian Church because I admired him so much.*

These claims are more believable, given Shields's lifelong connection to Lexington and the fact that the church where he served as trustee after the war had several members who had attended Jackson's class. Shields further claimed he was "indebted to General Jackson for his early religious training" and recalled that Jackson routinely called his name in prayer: "When he prayed, he would say, 'Remember Jeff.'" Henry Boley, in his nostalgic but dated look at early twentieth-century Lexington titled *Lexington in Old Virginia*, includes a sketch of Shields in his chapter "Colored Personalities": "Uncle Jeff, ebony in color, with his snow white beard, twinkling eye, high silk hat, and Prince Albert coat, was a sight as familiar on the street as the post office."

Shields's fame spread throughout Virginia, and he became a staple among many Lost Cause adherents. In 1906, another convert from Jackson's "colored Sabbath school," Dr. Lylburn Downing, unveiled a stained-glass window honoring Jackson at Fifth Avenue Presbyterian Church in Roanoke, Virginia. The dedication of the window made national news and was attended by many Confederate veterans, a number of prominent Roanoke citizens and members of the press. The keynote speaker for the event was none other than Jefferson Shields.

One letter on file at the Stonewall Jackson House in Lexington gives an account of an encounter that a Dr. Lewis Gravely Pedigo had with Jeff Shields in 1906:

> *He lived in Lexington, and had been the body servant of General Stonewall Jackson through his war time experiences. The Confederate veterans had made a pet and a hero of him. He used to attend all of their public meetings. They would pin badges, medals, and decorations on him and place him at the head of their processions with a beautiful flag…I believe, if he had been born in Central Africa, he would have been a king.*

It would be easy to conclude that the Confederate veterans were taking advantage of Shields's desire for fame and acceptance and making a "pet" of him for their own entertainment and purposes—and no doubt many of them were—but one could also conclude that it was Shields who actually gained the upper hand from this relationship, as his fame "assured him a comfortable income to the end of his earthly pilgrimage." So comfortable, in fact, that he purchased a lot on what is now Davidson Street in Lexington and built a handsome brick home that still stands. As Ervin Jordan has noted, "As intelligent human beings, they were sometimes able to manipulate the slavery system for their own purposes and obtain unprecedented opportunities." Though Shields's manipulation occurred postwar, it is, nonetheless, a classic example of Jordan's observation.

Jefferson Shields lived in Lexington with his wife, the former Mary McNutt, until his death in 1918 at the ripe old age of eighty-nine. Today, his

Jefferson Shields's headstone. *Photo by author.*

earthly remains, along with those of his wife, rest in Evergreen Cemetery in Lexington.

Unlike the claims of Jefferson Shields, fellow Lexingtonian Jim Lewis's service as Jackson's personal servant during the war has been established by numerous accounts of those who knew Lewis and served with Jackson. These accounts offer a remarkable glimpse into the two men's relationship, as well as a look at one slave's service in the Confederacy.

Lewis became attached to Jackson as his personal servant after Jackson arrived in Winchester, Virginia. Some historians have suggested that Lewis was a free black. W.G. Bean refers to Lewis as "a free negro of Lexington" in his biography of Sandie Pendleton. Yet Jackson biographer James Robertson points out that Jackson paid a Lexington resident by the name of "W.C. Lewis" monies "for hire." William C. Lewis was, along with Jackson, a member of Lexington Presbyterian Church. Lewis also served as an elder in the church. Though no known reference exists, it is possible that Jim Lewis had, like Jefferson Shields, attended Jackson's black Sunday school class, given the fact that records indicate he was the property of fellow church member W.C. Lewis.

Another payment was made a year later in the amount of $150 for the "hire of Jim." This would suggest that Jim Lewis was likely a slave owned by W.C. Lewis and was "leased" to Jackson during the war. Lewis's exact age is unknown. One source suggests he was "in the prime of life," and another claims he was about the same age as Jackson, while Robertson wrote that "he was in all likelihood in an advanced age at the time of the conflict."

Jackson staff member, Henry Kyd Douglas, provided this description of Lewis in his book *I Rode with Stonewall*:

> *The faithful fellow has become historical by reason of his association with General Jackson, to whom his devotion was a kind of superstition. He became important and was aware of it and never denied an anecdote told of him, however incredible, if the General was in it. He was a handsome mulatto, in the prime of life, well-made and with excellent manners, but perhaps altogether true only to the General.*

Douglas goes on to describe other, less flattering characteristics of Lewis, suggesting he was "fond of liquor" and "somewhat addicted to cards." That description is questionable, as Jackson had little patience for drunkenness and was not known to tolerate behavior he considered immoral within the close ranks of his command, much less someone as intimate with Jackson as Lewis. Moreover, Jackson's willingness to send Lewis on errands and "furloughs," unattended, casts further doubt on Douglas's description of Lewis.

Another staff officer, James Power Smith, wrote that Lewis, like Jackson, encouraged others to attend church and did so by practical example: "Over in Clarke County, Jim on Superior, at the head of a troop of our servants, affected the style of a general and staff, and went off, with hat in his hand, to some church for the colored people. I remember the general himself and the staff coming out of their tents to see the colored contingent go off in great style."

There is ample evidence that Lewis was close to Jackson and familiar with many of his personal habits, including Jackson's legendary prayer routine. On one occasion, when Jackson entered his tent to pray, Lewis held on to Little Sorrel's reins and raised his hand to the chattering crowd preparing to break camp. With a look of displeasure and a loud whisper, Lewis admonished, "Hush, the general is praying."

Lewis was also familiar with Jackson's habit of rising at "early dawn." A local citizen inviting Jackson to breakfast at the normal hour in the morning received this reply from Lewis: "Sh! You don't spec' to find the general here at this hour, do you? He left here 'bout midnight, and I spec' by this time he's whippin' Banks in the Valley." Lewis was usually the first to know something was afoot, stating that he "could always tell when a battle was near at hand by seeing the general get up a great many times in the night to pray." Henry Kyd Douglas wrote that when Lewis observed Jackson getting up in the middle of the night to pray, Lewis said, "I begin to cook rations and pack up for there will be hell to pay in the morning."

Jackson's trust of Lewis extended to his accepting Lewis's advice on at least one occasion. Once, when Jackson called for Lewis to bring Little Sorrel to him, Lewis protested, reminding Jackson that the horse had been ridden hard the previous day in battle. According to Mrs. Jackson, "An amusing war of words passed between them; but Jim had it in his power to gain the victory, and brought out another horse, which the general mounted." The fact that Jackson, who was infamous for his exacting expectations regarding orders, would tolerate a disagreement from a servant, especially when it came to something as important as to which horse he would be riding, indicates that the relationship went somewhat beyond that of master and

Little Sorrel, Stonewall Jackson's horse, postwar. *VMI Archives.*

slave. There was even a hint of jealousy among some staff members over the favored treatment Lewis received from Jackson. J.T.L. Preston once complained in a letter to his wife, "Now that Jim Lewis is going home on furlough, I cannot refrain from scribbling again. White people here have no chance of getting a furlough; it is only our colored friends who can escape for a time the evils of war."

Lewis was also closely attached to members of Jackson's staff. When Private William "Willy" C. Preston of the Fourth Virginia, and the son of Jackson's fellow Presbyterian Colonel J.T.L. Preston, was killed at Second Manassas, Lewis overheard Dr. McGuire reporting Preston's death to Jackson. Lewis was overcome with sorrow and he "rolled on the ground groaning, in his agony of grief." Frank Vandiver notes that Jim "knew and loved Willy as his own."

After Jackson's wounding at Chancellorsville on May 2, 1863, Jim Lewis would be one of Jackson's constant companions and comforters as Jackson slowly succumbed to his wounds. By 2:00 a.m. on May 3, Jackson was in the capable hands of Dr. McGuire. After amputating Jackson's arm, it was determined he had to be moved from the temporary tent hospital to a safer location. Jackson made the twenty-seven-mile trip by ambulance to Guiney Station. Jim Lewis followed behind "with horses, headquarters supplies, and Jackson's personal belongings."

Upon arriving at the estate of Thomas Coleman Chandler at Guiney Station, Dr. McGuire promptly limited access to Jackson. The only ones allowed in Jackson's room were McGuire, Joseph Graham Morrison, James Power Smith and Jim Lewis. Retiring for the evening, McGuire, Morrison and Smith all rested in the upper room of the cottage at the estate. Lewis slept closest to Jackson, in the room next to the wounded general. McGuire trusted Lewis to listen and watch for any sound or movement coming from Jackson's room. Lewis's care included fetching the general an occasional glass of cold milk from the Chandler home. Robertson notes that things initially seemed to be going well. "Vital signs looked good into Wednesday night. McGuire felt safe in leaving Jackson in the affectionate care of Jim Lewis…Lewis sat quietly and watched Jackson fall asleep."

When Jackson's condition worsened, the general's moaning woke Lewis, and he and Lacy rushed to Jackson's bedside. Jackson requested that a wet towel be applied to his left side, where he was experiencing severe pain. Lewis soaked a towel in cold spring water and applied the cool compresses to Jackson's side. The pain did not subside. Lewis became

William Nelson Pendleton, circa 1865. *Special Collections, Leyburn Library, Washington and Lee University.*

worried and tried for some time to get Jackson to allow him to call Dr. McGuire. Finally, at daybreak, Jackson instructed Lewis to wake McGuire. McGuire was startled from a deep sleep by Lewis's solemn words: "The general wants you." Lewis watched apprehensively as McGuire examined Jackson. McGuire was now convinced that pneumonia had set in.

Jackson's wife would later write, "Tears were shed over that dying bed by strong men who were unused to weep, and it was touching to see the genuine grief of his servant, Jim, who nursed him faithfully to the end." After Jackson's death, Jim Lewis would have the honor of leading Jackson's riderless horses during both of the general's funerals.

Though we don't know all the details, Lewis remained with the Stonewall Brigade after Jackson's death and "attached himself to [Sandie] Pendleton." Pendleton was one of Jackson's staff officers and the only son of Confederate general William Nelson Pendleton. This attachment is evidenced by the incident of Pendleton's wounding and subsequent death at the Battle of Fisher's Hill on September 22, 1864. Upon examining Pendleton, Dr. McGuire informed him that the wound in his abdomen was mortal. Pendleton succumbed to his wounds the evening of September 23, just five days before his twenty-fourth birthday.

The family was devastated. So was Lewis. Bean notes that after Sandie's death, Lewis was "borne down with grief and inconsolate." Henry Douglas also makes mention of Lewis's grief regarding the passing of Jackson and Sandie Pendleton: "When the General died Jim's honest grief was almost inconsolable. He then attached himself to Pendleton, but when he fell also Jim seemed to break down. He grew sad and went home on a short furlough, saying he would come back and join some one of the 'old staff,' Jackson's own. But he was taken ill and died in Lexington and lies buried in that historic town." James Robertson notes that Lewis's death was "in part presumably from grief."

Ten years after the war ended, "An Appeal to Stonewall Jackson's Old Command" for erecting a monument to Jim Lewis appeared in the *Lexington Gazette and Citizen*:

> *Let us not forget that James Lewis, General Jackson's faithful body servant, lies in a neglected grave in the Colored Cemetery at Lexington without a stone to record his deathless devotion to the General. Jim was with the General until his death, followed his body through Richmond and to Lexington, and then served the gallant Colonel Sandy Pendleton till his glorious death at Toms Brook. The writer met him bringing the Col's horse and baggage home bowed down with grief, inconsolable, but in apparently good health. We tried to cheer him up, but could only get for an answer, "Major de dear ole General's gone, and Mars Sandy and its Jim's time next," and sadly he went on his way to carry out Mars Sandy's last requests; and in a few days afterwards we passed his corpse going to the cemetery. He was faithful among the faithless in his devotion to and care of General Jackson, and deserves a monument at our hands, officers of the corps, and all who remember him will be received at the* Gazette *office.*

Lewis was buried in a Lexington cemetery that was segregated for blacks. This cemetery has quite an interesting history and originally encompassed an area bordered roughly by what are today North Lewis Street, Washington Street and Marble Lane. In 1880, Lexington established a new cemetery for African Americans known as Evergreen, which is where Jefferson Shields is buried. The remains of all who were interred in the original cemetery were purportedly moved to Evergreen. But there is some lingering doubt that the reinterment actually occurred. In a conversation with Megan Haley Newman, curator of the Stonewall Jackson House in 2004, Ms. Haley informed me that her research led her to believe that the contractor who did some of the excavating, and who was hired to move the remains, was perhaps not thorough in his work, and that many, if not most, of the remains had been left in their original graves. Of course, this could have been due more to the fact that the graves were poorly marked—if at all—as opposed to any disregard for those buried there. As recently as 2007, pieces of old marble headstones were discovered in this area, and a complete, intact headstone was moved by the City of Lexington to the Stonewall Jackson Memorial Cemetery for safekeeping. That headstone was afterward relocated—with appropriate wording on a small memorial—to Evergreen Cemetery.

By 1880, the original cemetery was filling rapidly and falling into neglect. Many of the dead were originally identified by simple wooden markers—long since rotted—and some weren't identified at all. Though records are somewhat sketchy, research seems to indicate that prospective white developers were as much an impetus for what happened next as were blacks concerned about the condition of the graves of their ancestors and loved ones.

Petitions from the community had been presented to the town council asking that the town move the "colored dead from the present burial ground" to a new site. Seeing an opportunity, local judge (and former Confederate officer) William McLaughlin made an offer to the town council to exchange six acres of property he owned just outside the town limits for a portion—approximately three acres—of the existing black burial ground. Apparently, some blacks opposed the plan and made it known that they wished to "express their views" on the subject. A motion to table the judge's offer and hear out the petitioners lost by one vote. Captain G.W. Pettigrew, a member of council who ran a local confectioners shop that sold shotguns as well as sweets, resigned in protest. The remaining members of council instructed a committee to meet with the town attorney and proceed with the exchange. Eventually, the black petitioners were heard, but to no avail. Evidently, the land exchange offered by the powerful Judge McLaughlin was a "done deal."

McLaughlin had already shown an unusually callous—even for those times—disregard for the concerns of Lexington blacks by being party to a legal threat against Stonewall Jackson in 1858 over Jackson's "colored Sabbath school," which McLaughlin considered "an unlawful assembly" when it was still illegal in Virginia to teach blacks to read. Ironically, McLaughlin would later give a dedication speech at Jackson's life-sized bronze statue unveiled over the Confederate general's grave in 1891—a statue that had been funded, in part, by some of Jackson's former black students.

As the year progressed, the town engineer enclosed the new cemetery, prepared an entrance and laid out the grounds for lots. In October 1880, the Lexington Town Council ordered that "further burial of the dead in

Statue of Stonewall Jackson, Stonewall Jackson Memorial Cemetery. *Photo by author.*

the old cemetery be discontinued." A month later, the council accepted the McLaughlin deed in exchange for a portion of the original black cemetery, with the Town of Lexington apparently retaining the remainder of the property. Lexington City Hall today borders the portion of the original cemetery obtained by McLaughlin.

The saga of the original cemetery ostensibly came to a close in the summer of 1881 with the appointment of a "Board of Trustees of competent colored people" supervised by the mayor and town council. The board administered the new cemetery (named "Evergreen"), sold lots and kept a "separate account" for operations. The new trustees included William Washington, William Drummond, Edmund W. White, James Humbles, James "Deacon" Jackson, William S. Harvey and Randall Talbott. Both Humbles and Jackson were free blacks before the war, and Humbles had actually served in the Confederate army.

James Jackson was a free black during the Civil War, a respected businessman and the town's most prominent barber, claiming that he had been Robert E. Lee's barber during Lee's years in Lexington. Local oral tradition and family history suggests Jackson and his son attended Stonewall Jackson's Sunday school class for slaves and free blacks. Records further indicate that he regularly petitioned council for permission to establish a bath in his barber shop. He built a home on Main Street (across from wartime Virginia governor Letcher's house) and was bold enough (considering the times) to complain to the town fathers when water ran off from Letcher's yard into his new home. The problem was fixed within the week.

In 1882, a local contractor was paid a substantial sum for his services in the cemetery, presumably for moving corpses from the old to the new site. Then, in June 1883, the street was widened in front of the judge's new property, and a portion was cut off the old cemetery property. It was noted that any bodies found were to be moved to the "new cemetery for colored people."

But were all the bodies moved? Fast-forward to 1946. The town of Lexington was hard-pressed for cash, and local officials were looking for ways to raise additional money. Governing costs were rising, and revenues were at a standstill. On September 19, the town council held a joint meeting with the trustees of the Evergreen Cemetery to consider the sale of what remained of the original cemetery property. The old cemetery was "long since abandoned" and a "vacant lot." The town attorney said that the property was a "liability" and was serving "no useful purpose and had to be kept cleaned up." Moreover, all the bodies had long ago been removed—or so the council was assured.

On September 25, 1946, the following public notice appeared in the *Lexington Gazette*: "Sale of Valuable Property by the Town of Lexington, Virginia." The legal description of one of the properties to be auctioned off included parts of the original African American cemetery and included the following covenant: "Should the remains of any person be found buried on said land, the Town of Lexington, at its own expense, will have the same re-interred by a local mortician in Evergreen Cemetery."

Clearly, this statement is indicative that there were suspicions that all of the bodies had not been removed, as some had indicated. This is where the story becomes controversial. According to some locals, sufficient care was not taken to make sure remains discovered were actually reinterred. One longtime Lexington African American resident related the following: "My family always said that a few shovels full of earth were taken from each grave to the new cemetery. It is doubtful that any skeletal remains were moved." Additionally, at least one stone was not moved. There are also local stories of dogs seen running through the streets carrying human bones after excavating had begun. One other longtime Lexington resident told the author that some bones had, in fact, been discovered during construction of a dwelling many years ago, and he thought these bones had been reinterred at Evergreen and also revealed that, as a young boy playing in the area, he and his friends referred to one particular spot as "dead man's gulch"—due to what they found there. He would elaborate no further.

My own investigation in 2007 revealed that the one headstone previously mentioned was still there in the backyard of one of the homes. While there, the landowner also revealed that she and her son had discovered a "tomb" on the property. To my knowledge, that has yet to be verified. Another landowner showed me a piece of yet another marble headstone and told me she had found what she believed to be human bones on her property. Again, I have no information confirming the validity of the latter claim. Nonetheless, all of this raises a number of questions: Were the remains of Jim Lewis, Stonewall Jackson's cook and servant during the war, ever reinterred? Why was the one headstone left? Did greed, both public and private, override proper respect and dignity for the dead, in addition to the historic significance of the original black cemetery? Are there still human remains lying unknown in this area of Lexington?

As previously noted, in December 1875, an anonymous Confederate veteran wrote to the local paper dismayed over the fact that Jim Lewis "lies in a neglected grave in the Colored Cemetery at Lexington without a stone." And according to an editorial published in 2008 in the *Rockbridge Advocate* by editor Doug Harwood, when Stonewall Jackson's statue was being erected in 1891, "an Englishman offered to pay for a monument to mark the grave of one of his slaves [Jim Lewis]. The town ignored his offer."

Also in 2008, city officials rejected a petition to help fund a Virginia historical highway marker that, along with describing the history of the cemetery, notes Lewis's association with Jackson and the fact that Lewis was buried in the old cemetery. The marker, approved by the Virginia Department of Historical Resources, was the result of an application submitted by me and two other individuals. However, at several public meetings, concern surfaced over the wording of the text for the marker due to the mention of Lewis and, more specifically, Jackson. Some members of the community felt that more blacks than just Lewis should be mentioned and that Jackson's name should not be mentioned at all. VDH however, required that a state historical marker reference a person of historical significance in the text that appears on the marker for a cemetery. At the time of the application, VDH's rule read as follows: "In the case of a cemetery, it must be listed on the state or national register or contain the grave of someone of state or national historical significance." It was my opinion that Jim Lewis met this benchmark. But the official I originally spoke with at VDH felt the marker would have a much better chance of approval if a specific mention of Stonewall Jackson were made. Thus, the following text was originally submitted and approved by VDH:

> *Near this spot is the original African American cemetery of Lexington. Dating to the days of slavery, this cemetery was abandoned in 1880 and the persons buried here were purportedly moved to Evergreen Cemetery. Jim Lewis, an African American who served as Thomas J. "Stonewall" Jackson's body servant and cook during the Civil War, was buried here. Soldiers knew a march was imminent when Lewis started packing the secretive general's baggage. Lewis's and other graves were unmarked and never identified. In 1946, the City of Lexington sold the old cemetery, and houses were built over the original burial ground.*

Even so, after being contacted by others in the community, and with my approval and that of the other applicants, VDH approved a rewording of the text, waiving its "someone of state or national historical significance" rule and excluding any reference to either Lewis or Jackson. Unfortunately, due to continual delays by city officials, the marker was ultimately placed outside Lexington city limits, off the U.S. Route 11 bypass and not near the original cemetery. Thus, Jim Lewis was, for the third time, denied any official recognition by the City of Lexington—despite his close connection to one of Lexington's favorite sons and service to the commonwealth. The text that ultimately appeared on the marker reads as follows:

> *Near the intersection of Washington and Lewis Streets stood the original burial ground for Lexington's substantial free black community and slaves dating to the early 1800s. The majority of the original burials were in unmarked graves and no records were maintained of these burials. The Town of Lexington obtained ownership of the cemetery in 1876 and closed it in 1880 and the persons buried there were purportedly moved to Evergreen Cemetery, although there is little information to document the extent of reburials. In 1946 the Town of Lexington subdivided the old cemetery and houses were built over the burial ground.*

So what were the results of Shields's and Lewis's service to the Confederate States of America and to the Commonwealth of Virginia? Regrettably, neither received the recognition they deserved. As Ervin Jordan observed, "Only in the reminiscences of ex-Confederates are body servants given any

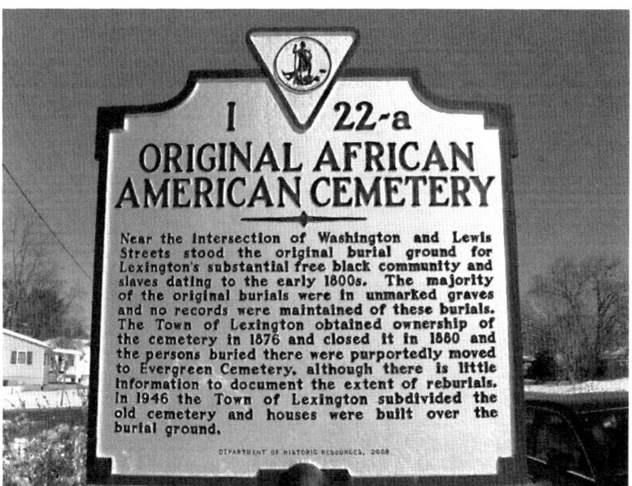

Highway marker for the African American cemetery. *Photo by author.*

sort of appreciation." It would appear that was precisely the case with Jim Lewis. No one else seems to care.

Ironically, both men are better remembered than most of the white Southern soldiers who fought for the South—for different reasons, of course. In the case of Jefferson Shields, his image is one of the best known of African American Confederates and has been distributed worldwide via the Internet. His service to the Confederacy contributed to his ability to earn a comfortable living after the war and to his status and acceptance among those Confederate veterans with whom he chose to associate. His wedding ceremony was performed by Stonewall Jackson's pastor, William S. White, and he received a decent burial. Today, his grave is marked by his original tombstone, as well as by a Veterans' Administration–issued marker noting his service in the Confederate army. The well-manicured cemetery in which he rests is maintained by the City of Lexington. But Shields died in 1918, six years before Virginia passed legislation granting pensions to blacks who had served in the Confederate army. Thus, he was denied the official recognition

Stonewall Jackson's Camp Prayer, originally sketched by Adalbert J. Volck, which served as the basis for an 1866 etching by J.C. Buttre. The African American kneeling to Jackson's right is believed to be Jim Lewis. *Museum of the Confederacy.*

and compensation he had earned for his service, even though that service was limited to "body servant" and cook.

Sadly, for Jim Lewis, his service yielded even less recognition. Though Lewis is as well known, if not better known, than Shields for his Confederate army service and his well-documented attachment to one of the South's most revered generals, there are no known photographs of him in existence, though most believe it is Lewis who is the African American depicted in Adalbert J. Volck's famous sketch of a prayer meeting in Jackson's camp. His fame did lead to a portrayal in the not-so-successful motion picture *Gods and Generals*. That may be a first for an African American Confederate. But Jim Lewis's end was not a happy one. He apparently died in a state of depression, loneliness and despair—utterly forgotten by both the men and government he served. The Confederates he served with such devotion—for whatever reasons—even failed to properly mark his grave, though some attempt was made toward that end after the war. Whatever was left of his final resting place was sold to developers and bulldozed, his dust likely becoming part of a house's foundation or his bones carried off by a dog. And despite other attempts to at least acknowledge Lewis's service and final resting place, he remains little more than a footnote and perhaps an uncomfortable reminder of America's most tragic era. Certainly, one who served the Commonwealth of Virginia—and one of its favorite sons with such allegiance—has earned a place of recognition in its history.

These two men—often used as pawns to support exaggerated claims by some, their service dismissed as irrelevant by others and largely forgotten by everyone else—are a regrettable postscript to what is already a regrettable era in America's history.

A lesser-known slave who lived in Rockbridge County and also served in the Confederate army was Levi Miller. Miller is distinct from both Shields and Lewis in that there is some evidence—as in the case of James Humbles—that he actually took up arms against the Union army rather than serving simply as a cook or "body servant." Reliable documentation of blacks actually fighting for the Confederacy is a rarity. But Ervin Jordan lends some credibility to the claim that Miller did, in fact, bear arms against the Yankees:

> *Miller received a full pension from Virginia as an ex-Confederate soldier and affectionately spoke of their wartime experiences as comrades in arms. "Levi Miller stood by my side and* [no] *man never fought any better that he did," wrote Captain J.E. Anderson, "and when the enemy tried to cross*

> *our little breastworks and we clubbed and bayonetted them off, no one used his bayonet with more skill and effect than Levi Miller."*

Jordan adds:

> *After his death on 25 February 1921, the* Winchester Evening Star *published a rhapsodic tribute: "Levi Miller, one of the few colored men regularly enlisted in the Confederate army during the Civil War…to enter the southern army and fight through the four entire years of war."*

However, Robert Moore's research regarding Miller's service has failed to turn up any record of this Levi Miller on a muster roll. Moore posts the following observation on his blog, "Cenantua's Blog":

> *The stories go, that he not only served, but fought … and was "enrolled as a full-fledged soldier" by "unanimous vote of the Texans." Yet, he isn't on the muster rolls.*

Moore noted in a subsequent post that there could be an explanation for this:

> *My thought is that he doesn't appear in the muster rolls for good reason… the Confederate government did not permit blacks to enlist as soldiers. They could be cooks, body servants, etc., but until late in the war, the option wasn't there. Miller was voted in as a regular member of his unit earlier in the war, he was acknowledged by the white soldiers, but he was not acknowledged by the government as a full-fledged soldier. He could not be recognized by the government, on the muster rolls, as it wasn't allowed.*
>
> *It's interesting, but this thought brings up something else. I think it lends something to the "rich man's war, poor man's fight" argument. Obviously, as in even modern cases of people in the military, the soldier does not believe in everything about his government. He may fight, but that doesn't mean he agrees with the government or all of its positions.*

Jordan notes that Miller did, nonetheless, receive a hero's burial complete with a Confederate flag draped over his coffin and was buried in its black cemetery (Evergreen).

Naturally, there were local slaves—as well as free blacks—who preferred helping the invading army rather than hindering it. One such incident

Headstone of Levi Miller. *Photo by author.*

involved a large store of arms. There are a number of accounts providing sometimes-conflicting details about several packet boats or "barges" that were loaded with ordnance from VMI with the intent of sending them downriver to Lynchburg in order to avoid capture by Hunter's invading army. Superintendent Smith gives his version of what was on the boats and what happened to them in a letter sent to Major General William H. Richardson, dated June 17, 1864:

> *I have brought with the command 4 Brass pieces, 2 rifle guns 3 in. and ammunition, and had privately disposed of the section of the Letcher Battery given to the Institute. The mountain Howitzers, ammunition and old cadet muskets were turned over to the Confederate authorities, and I hold the receipt of the commanding officer at Lexington for them. I understand they were caught above the break in the canal, and were destroyed or captured.*

General Hunter makes this statement in his official report dated August 8, 1864, regarding the raid on VMI: "6 barges laden with commissary stores,

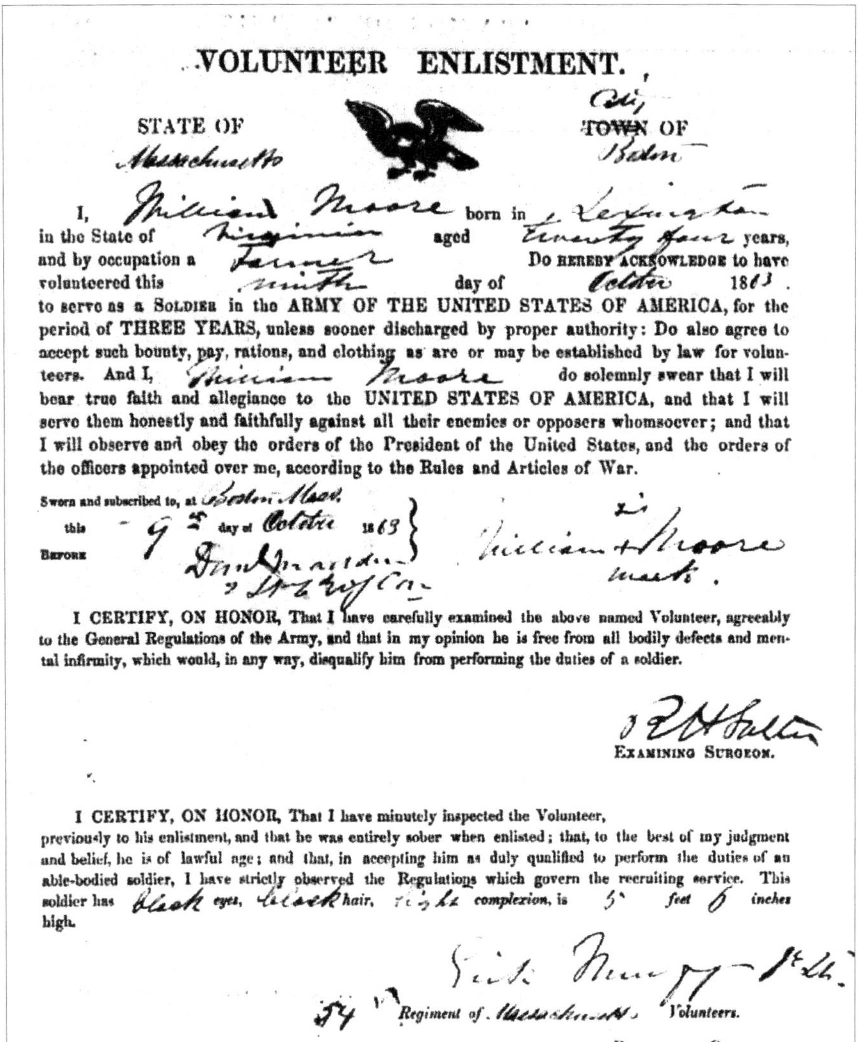

VOLUNTEER ENLISTMENT.

STATE OF Massachusetts — ~~TOWN~~ City OF Boston

I, William Moore born in Lexington in the State of Virginia aged twenty four years, and by occupation a Farmer Do HEREBY ACKNOWLEDGE to have volunteered this ninth day of October 1863, to serve as a SOLDIER in the ARMY OF THE UNITED STATES OF AMERICA, for the period of THREE YEARS, unless sooner discharged by proper authority: Do also agree to accept such bounty, pay, rations, and clothing as are or may be established by law for volunteers. And I, William Moore do solemnly swear that I will bear true faith and allegiance to the UNITED STATES OF AMERICA, and that I will serve them honestly and faithfully against all their enemies or opposers whomsoever; and that I will observe and obey the orders of the President of the United States, and the orders of the officers appointed over me, according to the Rules and Articles of War.

Sworn and subscribed to, at Boston Mass. this 9th day of October 1863 BEFORE [illegible]

William his mark Moore

I CERTIFY, ON HONOR, That I have carefully examined the above named Volunteer, agreeably to the General Regulations of the Army, and that in my opinion he is free from all bodily defects and mental infirmity, which would, in any way, disqualify him from performing the duties of a soldier.

[illegible signature]
EXAMINING SURGEON.

I CERTIFY, ON HONOR, That I have minutely inspected the Volunteer, previously to his enlistment, and that he was entirely sober when enlisted; that, to the best of my judgment and belief, he is of lawful age; and that, in accepting him as duly qualified to perform the duties of an able-bodied soldier, I have strictly observed the Regulations which govern the recruiting service. This soldier has black eyes, black hair, light complexion, is 5 feet 6 inches high.

[illegible signature]
54th Regiment of Massachusetts Volunteers.
RECRUITING OFFICER.

Like Samuel Kenney, Rockbridge County's William Moore also enlisted in 54th Massachusetts Colored Infantry. Moore's enlistment paperwork is rare, however, in that it identifies him specifically as born in Lexington, Virginia. *Compiled Military Service Records, courtesy of Robert Moore.*

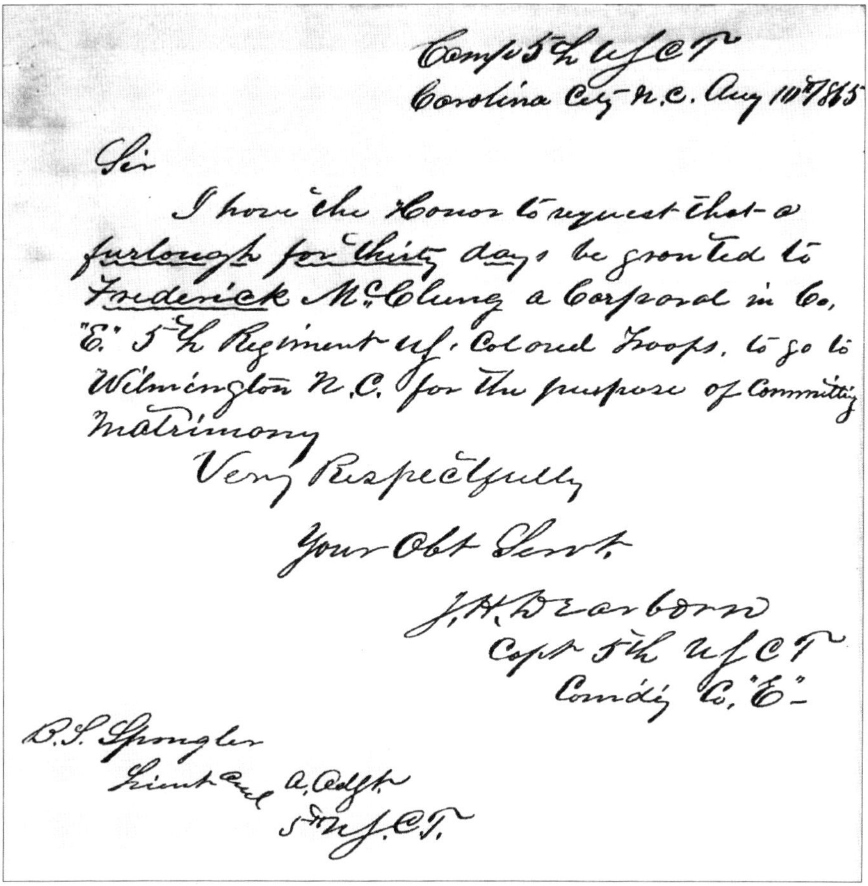
Camp 5th U.S.C.T.
Carolina City N.C. Aug 10th 1865

Sir

I have the Honor to request that a furlough for thirty days be granted to Frederick McClung a Corporal in Co. "E" 5th Regiment U.S. Colored Troops, to go to Wilmington N.C. for the purpose of Committing matrimony

Very Respectfully
Your Obt Servt.
J.H. Dearborn
Capt 5th U.S.C.T.
Comdg Co. "E"

B.S. Spengler
Lieut and A. Adjt
5th U.S.C.T.

Letter from Captain J.H. Dearborn requesting a furlough for Private Frederick McClung, of the 5th USCT Infantry, "for the purpose of committing matrimony" in Wilmington, North Carolina. *Compiled Military Service Records, courtesy of Robert Moore.*

struggle would be long and difficult, but through their local churches, the Freedmen's Bureau, fraternal organizations, entrepreneurship, family and a determined will to succeed, that day would come. But they had much less to begin to *build* than did their white counterparts who were in the process of *rebuilding*. It is an important distinction. They, too, had witnessed the destruction of Lexington. Some had rejoiced—understandably so. "An eye for an eye" was, no doubt, in the minds of many slaves as they saw the citizens of Lexington suffer injustice and humiliation at the hands of the Yankees. Other blacks—for various reasons—were, like their white masters, repulsed at what they had seen. Some felt an attachment to their home, even in bondage. As odd and ironic as it seems through our eyes today, and despite the evils of slavery, there was often what we would today consider an inexplicable closeness between blacks and whites in the slave South. Writing in the October 2007 edition of *Civil War Times*, Professor Peter Carmichael noted the following:

> *No one can ignore the overwhelming historical evidence of mutual closeness between blacks and whites within the Slave South…Contextualizing these expressions of animosity as well as love and respect are essential if we want to understand the broader patterns of thought and actions in the Old South.*

Chapter 6

A Consecrated Coronet of Sorrow

The Legacy Endures

Beautiless and bleak, it becomes lovely in its consecrated coronet of sorrow, and it wins the sympathy of the heart and of history.
—Abram J. Ryan

Father Abram J. Ryan was a Catholic priest and poet who, though christened "Abraham," insisted on being called "Abram" due to his intense dislike for President Lincoln. Though Ryan never formally joined the Confederate army, he did volunteer his services as a chaplain during the last two years of the war. But it wasn't until after the war that Abram J. Ryan became a household name in the South and was widely known as the "Poet-priest of the South." "The Conquered Banner" (1865) and "The Sword of Robert E. Lee" (1866) were Ryan's best-known poems, and throughout much of the South, schoolchildren were required to memorize these two poems until the middle of the twentieth century. It was also Ryan who popularized the term "Lost Cause" as a perspective of remembrance held by many Southerners.

One of Ryan's most hauntingly beautiful poems isn't quite as well known as the two previously mentioned. First published in January 1867 with no title, Ryan later altered it some and assigned to it the title "The South." Then, in 1869, an expanded third version became "The Southland." Ten years later, a final fourth version appeared under the title "A Land Without Ruins." As David O'Connell writes in his 2006 biography of Ryan, *Furl That Banner: The Life of Abram J. Ryan, Poet-Priest of the South*:

The poem was written to buoy the hopes of people living under Reconstruction and trying to come to grips with the losses they had suffered, whether of loved ones, homes, livestock, or property. Ryan was determined to see some good in all of this, and he assured his fellow Southerners that better days lay ahead…

A LAND WITHOUT RUINS

A land without ruins is a land without memories—
a land without memories is a land without history.
A land that wears a laurel crown may be fair to see;
but twine a few sad cypress leaves around the brow of any land,
and be that land barren, beautiless and bleak, it becomes lovely
in its consecrated coronet of sorrow, and it wins the sympathy of the heart
and of history. Crowns of roses fade—crowns of thorns endure.
Calvaries and crucifixions take deepest hold of humanity—
the triumphs of might are transient—they pass and are forgotten—
the sufferings of right are graven deepest on the chronicle of nations.

Yes give me the land where the ruins are spread,
And the living tread light on the hearts of the dead;
Yes, give me a land that is blest by the dust,
And bright with the deeds of the down-trodden just.
Yes, give me the land where the battle's red blast
Has flashed to the future the fame of the past;
Yes, give me the land that hath legends and lays
That tell of the memories of long vanished days;
Yes, give me a land that hath story and song!
Enshrine the strife of the right with the wrong!
Yes, give me a land with a grave in each spot,
And names in the graves that shall not be forgot;
Yes, give me the land of the wreck and the tomb;
There is grandeur in graves—there is glory in gloom;
For out of the gloom future brightness is born,
As after the night comes the sunrise of morn;
And the graves of the dead with the grass overgrown
May yet form the footstool of liberty's throne,
And each single wreck in the war path of might
Shall yet be a rock in the temple of right.

While the verses of "A Land Without Ruins" certainly would apply—in the hearts and minds of many Southerners—to much of the South after the Civil War, it seems to me particularly appropriate in describing Lexington, Virginia, after the war. Though Lexington was devastated and had seen direct destruction during the conflict, local citizens immediately began the dual tasks of rebuilding and remembering. But the winter of 1864 was particularly difficult for the citizens of Lexington and other parts of the Shenandoah Valley. The chaos and devastation to the local economy caused by the destruction of the war provoked an epidemic of lawlessness bordering on anarchy. Arsonists destroyed farm structures, thieves stole livestock and local businesses and homes were burglarized. Inflation and currency devaluation only added to the woes of locals. The year 1865 began with a brutal cold snap, with temperatures plummeting below zero throughout January and much of February. Both food and firewood became hard to come by. Union deserters hiding in the surrounding mountains posed a constant threat—at least in the minds of those who had witnessed their potential for destruction. Then came the news of Lee's surrender. Things immediately became worse. Robert Driver makes this observation regarding the impact of Lee's surrender:

> *Surrender unleashed another storm of lawlessness in the county* [and the town of Lexington]. *Houses were surrounded by bands of outlaws and deserters, black and white, who broke and took what they wanted. Horses, cattle and sheep were stolen. Armed robbery took place on roads.*

But Lexington's residents would not let themselves become victims. In response to the increased lawlessness, volunteers organized patrols and policed the county. William Gilham, whose house had been burned by Hunter's men, became chief of police. Returning home after the surrender, former Confederate soldiers quickly became active in the community—joining the law enforcement effort and resuming trades, businesses and farming.

As spring turned to summer, Federal authorities and local officials started cooperating in restoring order. Trains began running again, and packet boats were once again seen on the North River at Jordan's Point. In July, one of the first prominent citizens of Lexington to announce his support for secession, John Brockenbrough, reopened the Lexington

Robert E. Lee, circa 1865. *Special Collections, Leyburn Library, Washington and Lee University.*

Law School, and classes began anew at Washington College, VMI and other local schools. Though it would be many years before Lexington would return to its prewar glory, normalcy was slowly returning for many of its residents.

But in September 1865 something occurred that would, perhaps, have more of a lasting impact on Lexington than any singular event since Hunter's raid the year before. When Robert E. Lee unassumingly rode into town on a horse named Traveller at 3:00 p.m. on the afternoon of September 18, he was a very tired man. Tired of the long ride, tired of war, tired of politics, tired of thinking of what might have been. Lee's most famous biographer, Douglas Southall Freeman, gives his description of Lee's ride to Lexington in the four-volume *R.E. Lee*:

> *He rode slowly, for the way was long and the weather was hot. Early in the afternoon he stopped at the house of a friend and remained there overnight. The next day, the temperature still oppressive, he kept the same schedule. On the third afternoon, he reached the crest of the Blue Ridge, beyond which lay his future home. As he looked over into the Valley, was he thinking of Jackson and of Thorough Gap, of Sharpsburg and of Harpers Ferry…or of the college up among the hills, and of a peaceful union of all the states that religion and education would insure against a renewal of war? None can answer, but as he had put all his self-discipline into a determination to close his mind to the irrevocable past, is it not probable that his thought was of the future?*

And Lee's future, from the time he dismounted his faithful warhorse until the day he would die five years hence, would be Lexington, Virginia. At first, Lee was reluctant to accept Washington College's offer, delivered through Judge John Brockenbrough, to become president of Washington College—a school that would eventually honor Lee's leadership there by adding his name to that of Lee's personal hero, George Washington. Given Lee's admiration of and connection to Washington, that act seemed almost providential. Lee's initial thoughts are reflected in his letter to the trustees of Washington College, dated August 24, 1865:

> *Fully impressed with the responsibilities of the office, I have feared that I should be unable to discharge its duties to the satisfaction of the trustees or to the benefit of the Country. The proper education of youth requires not only great ability, but I fear more strength than I now possess.*

Lee had another concern, and he expressed it clearly in the same letter:

> *There is another subject which has caused me serious reflection, and is, I think, worthy of the consideration of the Board. Being excluded from the*

Above: Robert E. Lee on Traveller. *Special Collections, Leyburn Library, Washington and Lee University.*

Left: Robert E. Lee, circa 1869. *Special Collections, Leyburn Library, Washington and Lee University.*

> *terms of amnesty in the proclamation of the President of the U.S., of the 29th May last, and an object of censure to a portion of the Country, I have thought it probable that my occupation of the position of President might draw upon the College a feeling of hostility; and I should, therefore, cause injury to an Institution which it would be my highest desire to advance. I think it the duty of every citizen, in the present condition of the Country, to do all in his power to aid in the restoration of peace and harmony, and in no way to oppose the policy of the State or General Government directed to that object. It is particularly incumbent on those charged with the instruction of the young to set them an example of submission to authority, and I could not consent to be the cause of animadversion upon the College.*

Nonetheless, Lee left the door open if the trustees, having acknowledged Lee's full disclosure, still wanted him:

> *Should you, however, take a different view, and think that my services in the position tendered to me by the Board will be advantageous to the College and Country, I will yield to your judgment and accept it; otherwise, I must most respectfully decline the office.*

Fortunately for all involved, including Lee, Washington College, Lexington, the South, the United States and the hundreds of young men he would influence, the trustees still wanted Lee as their president. Freeman explains:

> *As the trustees promptly relieved General Lee of all instructional duty, and expressed their agreement with his views, the question of his future work was quickly settled. The effect on Lee was immediate. Idleness and uncertainty were at an end. He had a task and he would discharge it. In his correspondence he began to set even more vigorously than before the example he thought the South required. He may have been prompted also to a more positive course because he saw the gloomy portents of the troubled times.*

Lee was accustomed to lost causes. It seemed as though he felt a kindred spirit to the broken-down college in the sleepy little village. They had much in common. The war had crippled Virginia's economy and, along with it, the prospects of Washington College. The school's buildings and library had suffered extensive damage and pillaging during Union general David Hunter's raid in June 1864. Only four of the school's professors remained, and the student body had dwindled to forty young men. Though the school's rich history included an endowment of stock by George Washington, its outlook seemed rather dismal. But Lee's efforts would, nonetheless, have a dramatic impact on the student body of Washington College, and his influence has echoed through subsequent generations. One of Lee's former students, C.W. Hedger, wrote:

> *Of all men I have ever known, I think General R.E. Lee by far the greatest example as a soldier, a citizen…and a Christian gentleman. As President, he displayed distinguished ability, showing his greatness of soul not only by refusing many far more lucrative positions that he might be of more benefit to the rising generation, but also by his interest in all the students, financing some of them through college, and looking after the physical, mental, moral, and spiritual welfare.*

Upon taking the helm of Washington College, Lee would embark on a task that would mean following advice he had given to a member of his staff at Appomattox:

> *You must remember we are a Christian people. For us as a Christian people there is but one course to pursue. We must accept the situation; these men must go home and plant a crop and we must proceed to build up our country on a new basis.*

The crop Lee would plant and cultivate would be the young men of Washington College. And Lee's Christian faith would be manifested in one of his first official acts as president of Washington College: ordering the construction of a chapel. No book about Lexington would be complete without some mention of this hauntingly historic and charming structure. It was early in 1866 that Lee recommended to the board of trustees that the original chapel room be converted to classroom use and that the board allocate funds for a new chapel building. Minutes from a meeting of the Committee on Buildings and Grounds in July 1866 indicate that after considering several alternatives, it was believed "best to return to the original idea of President Lee" and that "it should be a separate building of characteristic architecture, devoted exclusively to religious worship and instruction." The trustees' minutes also note that the committee submitted "a plan prepared by President Lee." On July 18, the trustees authorized the construction of the chapel "not to exceed $10,000." That cost restriction was removed at a later meeting.

Lee Chapel. *Photo by author.*

Construction began in 1867. Once completed, it quickly became central to much of student life on campus.

Lee Chapel resembles no other building on campus. It's Victorian and Romanesque architecture truly sets it apart from any other structure at the school. Some believe that John Renwick's 1847 design of the Smithsonian in Washington served, at least in part, as inspiration for the chapel's design. There are obvious similarities.

English ivy adorns much of the outer brick walls, and tradition has it that the ivy was originally brought from George Washington's tomb at Mount Vernon. Lee's connection to Washington, which he was conscious of and cultivated in his own life, continues in death.

Upon entering Lee Chapel, one immediately faces a commemorative marble plaque that memorializes the Liberty Hall Volunteers. Of course, the centerpiece and most striking item in Lee Chapel is Edward Valentine's *Recumbent Lee*. The simple dignity of the memorial won it wide acclaim as soon as it was unveiled, and today it is recognized as one of the finest monuments in marble ever created. The statue represents General Lee asleep in his tent after a battle and seems to reflect a statement Lee once made to Valentine: "I would like to go to some quiet place in the country and rest."

The chapel contains a number of other notable works of art, including the original Peale portraits of Washington and Lafayette, formerly at Mount Vernon. The Washington portrait once hung in Arlington House but was removed by the Lees in 1861 for fear that the Union soldiers would steal it.

From the chapel, one winds down a set of stairs to a state-of-the-art museum in the lower level that includes Lee's office, a portrait gallery displaying the Washington-Custis-Lee Collection, an exhibition tracing the history and heritage of Washington and Lee University and a museum shop. Lee's office remains as it was the last time he was there on September 28, 1870. The remainder of the lower level was converted to a museum in 1928 and contains many items once owned by the Lee and Washington families. The eclectic collection includes locks of both George Washington's and Robert E. Lee's hair. The Lee family crypt is also in the lower level; here are buried Robert E. Lee, his mother, his father (Light Horse Harry Lee), his wife and his children, along with other members of the Lee family. You will find that often visitors leave flowers or flags as memorials to General Lee.

During Lee's tenure, the downstairs of the chapel contained his office, the treasurer's office and a student center run by the YMCA (organized at Lee's suggestion in 1867), which became the university library, with its

Liberty Hall Volunteers Reunion, circa 1910. *Special Collections, Leyburn Library, Washington and Lee University.*

5,800 volumes, from 1869 to 1882. A marble plaque marks the original burial site of Robert E. Lee. Despite common misperception, Lee was never buried in or under the statue upstairs. The statue was designed as a memorial to Lee after his death. He was originally buried under the floor of the current museum, which was then the college library, until the addition to Lee Chapel was completed in 1883 and he was reburied in the crypt. Outside the chapel's basement glass doors are the buried remains of Traveller. Traveller was purchased by Lee in 1862 for $175 in gold. His faithful companion throughout the Civil War, Traveller became a well-known figure on the campus of Washington College. He lived in the custom-built stable next to the president's house, which now serves as the garage to the Lee House.

In Marshall Fishwick's wonderful mini biography of General Lee, titled *Lee After the War*, Fishwick writes, "Offices are silent biographies of those who spend much of their lives in them."

As Robert E. Lee's office was in the basement of Lee Chapel, that office, along with Lee Chapel itself, serves as a silent biography of General Lee as

Left: Robert E. Lee's crypt. *Photo by author.*

Below: Traveller's grave. *Author's collection.*

he spent, both literally and figuratively, much of his later life at the chapel. And you cannot really fully understand one without understanding the other.

So what was Lee's office like on the last day he occupied it? The room is simple, fifteen by eighteen feet, and originally had a simple pine floor of random widths. Only one item adorned the walls: a map of Augusta County, drawn by Jedediah Hotchkiss, Stonewall's mapmaker. There were no other prints or decorations. There was a small cast-iron stove attached to the fireplace in the corner. The room was painted white.

The furnishings were not elaborate. The largest item in the room is a bookcase that originally served as a sideboard, given to Lee by an admiring Virginia lady. Included in the bookcase are worn copies of *Webster's Dictionary*; French, English and Greek grammar books; and an algebra book. All show the telltale signs of frequent use. There is also a copy of the book *Our Children in Heaven* by William Holcombe, published in 1868. Lee knew something about that subject, having lost a daughter to typhoid during the war.

On the fireplace mantel were three faded pictures: George Peabody, who was a Northern friend of Lee; an unidentified Confederate family; and a picture of George Washington. Beside the large round table that served as Lee's desk is a large wicker basket, hand woven and given to Lee by a black Lexington woman. All of the chairs are simple, with wicker seats; there was a Victorian walnut secretary, a leather couch (a gift) and an end table on which sat an oil lamp. Lee's leather chair, another gifted item, is at the table. The table-desk is veneered with a glass top, with pens, ink, papers and other items neatly arranged.

This austere room was the command center of the school and Lee's administration. Here he planned the school's activities, admonished wayward students and convened counsels of advice with his colleagues. Here he spent many hours of solitude contemplating his past and his present charge.

Lee's daily practice was to rise early and have his private devotions and prayers, then prayers with his family at breakfast. After breakfast, Lee would walk the short distance to the chapel and always arrived promptly at 7:45 a.m. for the service. The service began 8:00 a.m. He would then descend to the lower level and to his office.

The legacy of Lee Chapel continues. Every year, on October 12, the anniversary of Lee's death, the chapel's bells toll nineteen times, matching the nineteen- gun salute given to an officer of Lee's rank and reminding everyone in Lexington of the solemn moment. Every year, the Sons of Confederate Veterans holds memorial services in the chapel on the Saturday following Lee-Jackson Day. Each year, the university honors Lee's birthday, January 19, with a Founder's Day program.

Today, Lee Chapel remains one of the true gems in Lexington and has been called the "Shrine of the South." Filled with its tradition and heritage, Lee Chapel remains a gathering place for lectures, memorial services, concerts and, yes, a place for spiritual reflection. Lee Chapel sees approximately sixty thousand visitors annually and continues to preserve Lee's legacy of honor, civility and faith, as well as his hope for the future.

It represents, perhaps more than any other single structure in Lexington, not only the *rebuilding* that the citizens of Lexington accomplished after the devastation of the Civil War, but also the *remembering*. Thus, the same man who was at the heart of the republic's divide and destruction left a symbolic legacy that endures in representing its rebuilding and unification. And in this rebuilding and remembering, Lexington continues to tread light on the hearts of the dead.

Bibliography

Allan, Elizabeth Preston. *The Life and Letters of Margaret Junkin Preston.* Boston: Houghton Mifflin, 1903.

Bean, W.G. *The Liberty Hall Volunteers: Stonewall's College Boys.* Charlottesville: University Press of Virginia, 1964.

———. *Stonewall's Man: Sandie Pendleton.* Chapel Hill: University of North Carolina Press, 1959.

Boley, Henry. *Lexington in Old Virginia.* 1936. Reprint, Lexington, VA: Liberty Hall Press, 1974.

Bostick, Douglas W. *Memorializing Robert E. Lee: The Story of Lee Chapel.* Charleston, SC: Joggling Board Press, 2005.

Bruce, Philip Alexander. *Brave Deeds of Confederate Soldiers.* 1916. Reprint, Stuarts Draft, VA: Virginia Gentleman Books, 1999.

Carmichael, Peter S. *The Last Generation, Young Virginians in Peace, War, and Reunion.* Chapel Hill, NC: University of North Carolina Press, 2005.

Chambers, Lenoir. *Stonewall Jackson and the Virginia Military Institute: The Lexington Years.* Lexington, VA: Garland Gray Memorial Research Center Stonewall Jackson House, 1982.

Compiled Service Records of Confederate Soldiers Who Served in Organizations from the State of Virginia. NARA microfilm publication M324A. War Department Collection of Confederate Records, Record Group 109. National Archives and Records Administration, Washington, D.C.

Coulling, Mary Price. *Margaret Junkin Preston: A Biography.* Winston-Salem, NC: John F. Blair, 1993.

Couper, William. *One Hundred Years at VMI.* 4 vols. Richmond, VA: Garrett and Massie, 1939

DeLaney, Theodore C. "Aspects of Black Religious and Educational Development in Lexington, Virginia, 1840–1928." *Proceedings of the Rockbridge Historical Society* 10 (1983): 139–51.

Dooley, Edwin L. "Gilt Buttons and the Collegiate Way: Francis H. Smith as Antebellum Schoolmaster." *Virginia Cavalcade* 36 (Summer 1986): 33.

Douglas, Henry Kyd. *I Rode with Stonewall.* Chapel Hill: University of North Carolina Press, 1940.

Doyle, Thomas S. "Some Recollections of Stonewall Jackson by One of His Sunday School Pupils." *Columbia* [South Carolina] *State*, n.d. Courtesy of the Stonewall Jackson House, Lexington, Virginia.

Driver, Robert J., Jr. *First Virginia Calvary*. Virginia Regimental Histories Series. Lynchburg, VA: H.E. Howard, Inc., 1991.

———. *Lexington and Rockbridge County in the Civil War.* Lynchburg, VA: H.E Howard, Inc., 1989.

Fishwick, Marshall W. *Lee After the War*. New York: Dodd, Mead & Company, 1963.

Flood, Charles Bracelen. *Lee—The Last Years.* New York: Mariner Books, 1998.

Freeman, Douglas Southall. *R.E. Lee.* Vols. I–IV. New York: Charles Scribner's Sons, 1935, 1936.

Hunter, Robert F. *Lexington Presbyterian Church, 1789–1989*. Lexington, VA: Lexington Presbyterian Church, 1991.

Jackson, Mary Anna. *Life and Letters of Stonewall Jackson—By His Wife*. 1892. Reprint, Harrisonburg, VA: Sprinkle, 1995.

Jordan, Ervin L., Jr. *Black Confederates and Afro-Yankees in Civil War Virginia.* Charlottesville: University Press of Virginia, 1995.

Junkin, D.X. *The Reverend George Junkin, D.D. LL.D.: A Historical Biography* Philadelphia: J.B. Lippincott & Co., 1871

Kennedy, Billy. *The Scots-Irish in the Shenandoah Valley.* Greenville, SC: Emerald House Group, Inc., 1996.

Koons, Kenneth E., William C. Davis, Emmert F. Bittinger, Stephen L. Longenecker, Jonathan M. Berkey, Nancy T. Sorrells and Jonathan A. Noyalas, contributors. *Home Front to Front Line: The Civil War Era in the Shenandoah Valley*. New Market, VA: Shenandoah Valley Battlefields Foundation, 2009.

Lee, Susan P. *Memoirs of William Nelson Pendleton, D.D.* 1893. Reprint, Harrisonburg, VA: Sprinkle, 1991.

MacDonald, Rose Moritmer Ellzey. *Mrs. Robert E. Lee.* 1939. Reprint, Stuarts Draft, VA: American Foundation Publications, 1998.

McDonald, Cornelia Peake. *A Woman's Civil War: A Diary with Reminiscences of the War, from March 1862.* Edited by C. Gwin Minrose. Madison: University of Wisconsin Press, 1992.

McGuire, Hunter Holmes. "Death of Stonewall Jackson." *Southern Historical Society Papers* 14 (1886).

McKim, Randolph H. *A Soldier's Recollections: Leaves from the Diary of a Young Confederate.* 1910. Reprint, Harrisonburg, VA: Sprinkle 1996.

Morton, Oren F. *A History of Rockbridge County, Virginia.* 1920. Reprint, Baltimore, MD: Regional Publishing Company, 1980.

Official Records of the Union and Confederate Armies (O.R.). Series 1, vol. 37/1, [S#70]. *The Lynchburg Campaign. No. 1., Reports of Maj. Gen. David Hunter, U.S. Army, commanding Department of West Virginia, including operations June 2–July 14.* Washington, D.C.: Government Printing Office, 1864.

Opie, John N. *A Rebel Cavalryman with Lee, Stuart and Jackson.* Chicago: W.B. Conkey Company, 1899.

Riley, Franklin L. *General Robert E. Lee after Appomattox.* New York: MacMillan Company, 1930.

Robertson, James I., Jr. *The Stonewall Brigade.* Baton Rouge: Louisiana State University Press, 1962.

———. *Stonewall Jackson: The Man, the Soldier, the Legend.* New York: Macmillan, 1997.

Shelor, Kathleen. "A Memorial to Stonewall Jackson—Stained Glass Window in Roanoke Church, Depicting Hero's Last Words, Recalls Tragedy of 73 Years Ago Today." *Richmond Times-Dispatch,* May 10, 1936.

Smith, Francis H. *History of the Virginia Military Institute.* Lynchburg, VA: J.P. Bell, 1912.

Strother, David Hunter. *A Virginia Yankee in the Civil War—The Diaries of David Hunter Strother.* Edited by Cecil Eby Jr. Chapel Hill: University of North Carolina Press, 1961.

Turner, Charles W. *Ted Barclay, Liberty Hall Volunteers: Letters from the Stonewall Brigade.* Berryville, VA: Rockbridge Publishing Company, 1992.

Vandiver, Frank E. *Mighty Stonewall.* 1957. Reprint, College Station: Texas A&M University Press, 1974.

Walker, Gary C. *Hunter's Fiery Raid Through Virginia Valleys.* Roanoke, VA: A&W Enterprises, 1989.

Webb, James. *Born Fighting: How the Scots-Irish Shaped America.* New York: Broadway Books, 2004.

White, William Spottswood. *Rev. William S. White, D.D., and His Times (1800–1873): An Autobiography*. Richmond, VA: Presbyterian Committee of Publication, 1891.

Williams, Richard G. *The Maxims of Robert E. Lee for Young Gentlemen*. Gretna, LA: Pelican Publishing Company, 2006.

———. *Stonewall Jackson: The Black Man's Friend*. Nashville, TN: Cumberland House, 2006.

Wise, Henry A. *Drawing Out the Man: The VMI Story*. Charlottesville: University Press of Virginia, 1978.

Wise, Jennings C. *Sunrise of the Virginia Military Institute as a School of Arms*. Lexington, VA, 1958.

Online Sources

Mckay, Brett, and Kate Mckay. "Manly Honor Part V: Honor in the American South" Art of Manliness. http://artofmanliness.com/2012/11/26/manly-honor-part-v-honor-in-the-american-south.

Southern Historical Society Papers Richmond, Virginia. http://www.archive.org.

Virginia Military Institute Archives. "General David Hunter and the Burning of VMI, June 1864." http://www.vmi.edu/archives/home.

Washington and Lee University. Robert E. Lee Collection. http://home.wlu.edu/~stanleyv/pentrans.htm.

Unpublished Resources

Newman, Megan Haley. "The African-American Experience in Thomas 'Stonewall' Jackson's Lexington." Stonewall Jackson House, Lexington, VA, 1994.

Pearson, E. Lynn. "Thy Kingdom Come: The Evangelical Stewards of Antebellum Lexington, 1851–1861." Stonewall Jackson House, Lexington, VA, 1989.

Wineman, Bradford Alexander. "Francis H. Smith: Architect of Antebellum Southern Military Schools and Educational Reform." PhD diss., Texas A&M University, 2006.

Withrow Scrapbooks. Vols. 7 & 16. Leyburn Library Special Collections, Washington and Lee University, Lexington, VA.

Newspapers

Lexington Gazette and Citizen, June 13, 1861; December 17, 1875.

Robert Moore's Sources

Barred and Disallowed Case Files of the Southern Claims Commission, 1871–1880. National Archives Microfilm Publication M1407, 4829 fiche. Records of the U.S. House of Representatives, Record Group 233. National Archives, Washington, D.C.

Compiled Military Service Records of Volunteer Union Soldiers Who Served with the United States Colored Troops: Artillery Organizations. M1818, 299 rolls. Records of the Adjutant General's Office, 1780s–1917, Record Group Number 94. National Archives, Washington, D.C.

Compiled Military Service Records of Volunteer Union Soldiers Who Served with the United States Colored Troops: 55th Massachusetts Infantry (Colored). M1801, 16 rolls. Records of the Adjutant General's Office, 1780s–1917, Record Group Number 94. National Archives, Washington, D.C.

Compiled Military Service Records of Volunteer Union Soldiers Who Served with the U.S. Colored Troops, 54th Massachusetts Infantry Regiment (Colored). M1898, 20 rolls. Records of the Adjutant General's Office, 1780s–1917, Record Group Number 94. National Archives, Washington, D.C.

Compiled Military Service Records of Volunteer Union Soldiers Who Served with the United States Colored Troops: 1st through 5th United States Colored Cavalry, 5th Massachusetts Cavalry (Colored), 6th United States Colored Cavalry. M1817, 107 rolls. Records of the Adjutant General's Office, 1780s–1917, Record Group Number 94. National Archives, Washington, D.C.

Compiled Military Service Records of Volunteer Union Soldiers Who Served with the United States Colored Troops: 1st U.S. Colored Infantry, 1st South Carolina Volunteers (Colored) Company A, 1st U.S. Colored Infantry (1 Year). M1819, 19 rolls. Records of the Adjutant General's Office, 1780s–1917, Record Group Number 94. National Archives, Washington, D.C.

Compiled Military Service Records of Volunteer Union Soldiers Who Served with the United States Colored Troops, Infantry Organizations.

M1822, 105 rolls. Records of the Adjutant General's Office, 1780s–1917, Record Group Number 94. National Archives, Washington, D.C.

Compiled Service Records of Volunteer Union Soldiers Who Served with the United States Colored Troops: Infantry Organizations, 8th through 13th, including the 11th (new). M1821, 109 rolls. Records of the Adjutant General's Office, 1780s–1917, Record Group Number 94. National Archives, Washington, D.C.

Compiled Military Service Records of Volunteer Union Soldiers Who Served with the United States Colored Troops: Infantry Organizations, 41st through 46th. M1994, 113 rolls. Records of the Adjutant General's Office, 1780s–1917, Record Group Number 94. National Archives, Washington, D.C.

Compiled Military Service Records of Volunteer Union Soldiers Who Served with the United States Colored Troops: Infantry Organizations, 47th through 55th. M2000, 183 rolls. Records of the Adjutant General's Office, 1780s–1917, Record Group Number 94. National Archives, Washington, D.C.

Compiled Military Service Records of Volunteer Union Soldiers Who Served with the United States Colored Troops, 2nd through 7th Colored Infantry including 3rd Tennessee Volunteers (African Descent), 6th Louisiana Infantry (African Descent) and 7th Louisiana Infantry (African Descent). M1820, 116 rolls. Records of the Adjutant General's Office, 1780s–1917, Record Group Number 94. National Archives, Washington, D.C.

Compiled Military Service Records of Volunteer Union Soldiers Who Served with the United States Colored Troops: Infantry Organizations, 31st through 35th. M1992, 86 rolls. Records of the Adjutant General's Office, 1780s–1917, Record Group Number 94. National Archives, Washington, D.C.

Compiled Military Service Records of Volunteer Union Soldiers Who Served with the United States Colored Troops: Infantry Organizations, 36th through 40th. M1993, 116 rolls. Records of the Adjutant General's Office, 1780s–1917, Record Group Number 94. National Archives, Washington, D.C.

Compiled Military Service Records of Volunteer Union Soldiers Who Served with the United States Colored Troops: Infantry Organizations, 20th through 25th. M1823, 98 rolls. Records of the Adjutant General's Office, 1780s–1917, Record Group Number 94. National Archives, Washington, D.C.

Compiled Military Service Records of Volunteer Union Soldiers Who Served with the United States Colored Troops: Infantry Organizations, 26th through 30th, Including the 29th Connecticut (Colored). M1824, 108 rolls. Records of the Adjutant General's Office, 1780s–1917, Record Group Number 94. National Archives, Washington, D.C.

Southern Claims Commission Approved Claims, 1871–1880: Virginia. National Archives Microfilm Publication M2094, 45 rolls. Records of the Accounting Officers of the Department of the Treasury, Record Group 217; National Archives, Washington, D.C.

Index

About the Author

Richard G. Williams Jr. is a southern writer, relic hunter, autodidact and raconteur who specializes in Virginia history and the War Between the States. A former contributor to the *Washington Times*' Civil War column, he has also written for *Homeschooling Today Magazine*, *Confederate Veteran*, *Western & Eastern Treasures Magazine* and regularly contributes articles about the Civil War and Virginia history to various publications and websites. He has co-produced two history-related videos: the award-winning *Institute on the Constitution* and *Still Standing: The Stonewall Jackson Story*. His writing and historical research involving the Confederacy earned him the Jefferson Davis Historical Gold Medal from the United Daughters of the Confederacy—the highest honor bestowed on non-members. Williams was born and grew up on battlefields in Virginia's rural Shenandoah Valley. He is a direct descendant of three Confederate soldiers and is a ninth-generation great-grandson of the Reverend Roger Williams.

Williams is actively involved in his community, having coached youth basketball, founding a 4H Club and serving as a Sunday school teacher for over thirty-three years. Concerned with preserving Virginia's rich historic heritage, Williams is a member of the Civil War Preservation Trust, the Museum of the Confederacy, the Sons of Confederate Veterans, the Waynesboro Heritage Foundation, and the Archeological Society of Virginia. He has co-authored the text for two of Virginia's historical highway markers and currently serves on the board of trustees for the National Civil War Chaplains Museum in Lynchburg, Virginia, and on the Battle of

Waynesboro (VA) Committee and is a member of the Artifact Detecting Team, as well as the Task Force for Metal Detecting Rights Foundation. The author of *Christian Business Legends*, *The Maxims of Robert E. Lee for Young Gentlemen* and *Stonewall Jackson: The Black Man's Friend*, Williams lives with his wife and family in Virginia's hallowed and storied Shenandoah Valley. When not working, reading, blogging or spending time with his lovely wife or any of his sixteen grandchildren, he can usually be found traipsing through some remote hollow in the Blue Ridge Mountains or some mist-covered battlefield here in Virginia, enjoying the company of his ancestors' spirits with a metal detector in his hands, a gleam in his eye and a smile on his face.

About the Contributor

A native and resident of the Shenandoah Valley, Robert H. Moore II has been writing about the American Civil War and other topics relevant to the history of the Shenandoah Valley for over twenty-five years. In addition to a number of magazine and newspaper articles, he has also published twelve books for various publishers, including seven works for H.E. Howard's Virginia Regimental Histories Series and his most recent work, *Tragedy in the Shenandoah Valley* (2006), published by The History Press. He is also the author of "Cenantua's Blog," which frequently taps into subjects that tie to his family roots in both the Shenandoah and Cumberland Valleys. He holds a master's degree in history from Old Dominion University and master's in technical communication from James Madison University. Moore currently works for the U.S. Department of Justice and in his spare time proudly volunteers, along with his daughters, at Harpers Ferry National Historic Park. He is currently working on a book about Southern Unionism in the Civil War.

Visit us at
www.historypress.net

This title is also available as an e-book